MW01635723

SHAKESPEARE

HAMLET

REVIEW QUESTIONS & ANSWERS

COLES EDITORIAL BOARD

Publisher's Note

Otabind (Ota-bind). This book has been bound using the patented Otabind process. You can open this book at any page, gently run your finger down the spine, and the pages will lie flat.

ABOUT COLES NOTES

COLES NOTES have been an indispensible aid to students on five continents since 1948.

COLES NOTES are available for a wide range of individual literary works. Clear, concise explanations and insights are provided along with interesting interpretations and evaluations.

Proper use of COLES NOTES will allow the student to pay greater attention to lectures and spend less time taking notes. This will result in a broader understanding of the work being studied and will free the student for increased participation in discussions.

COLES NOTES are an invaluable aid for review and exam preparation as well as an invitation to explore different interpretive paths.

COLES NOTES are written by experts in their fields. It should be noted that any literary judgement expressed herein is just that – the judgement of one school of thought. Interpretations that diverge from, or totally disagree with any criticism may be equally valid.

COLES NOTES are designed to supplement the text and are not intended as a substitute for reading the text itself. Use of the NOTES will serve not only to clarify the work being studied, but should enhance the readers enjoyment of the topic.

ISBN 0-7740-3197-2

COLES PUBLISHING COMPANY
TORONTO - CANADA
PRINTED IN CANADA

Manufactured by Webcom Limited
Cover finish: Webcom's Exclusive **DURACOAT**

CONTENTS

Part A: The Play in Brief

Introduction

As enjoyable and important as Shakespeare's plays are, they can be difficult to read. Since Shakespeare wrote his plays to appeal to Elizabethan audiences, much of the text is dated and means little to the average reader of today.

We are, therefore, presenting the substance of the play in readable form by eliminating, as much as possible, the outdated passages and by paraphrasing the more complicated ones. This will give you a better understanding and appreciation of the play, and will make the questions and answers more meaningful.

CHARACTERS IN THE PLAY

Claudius: King of Denmark
Hamlet: Son of the late king and nephew of the present king
Polonius: Lord chamberlain.
Horatio: Hamlet's friend.
Laertes: Polonius' son.

Voltimand
Cornelius
Rosencrantz
Guildenstern
Osric
A gentleman
} Courtiers.

A priest

Marcellus
Bernardo
} Officers.

Francisco: A soldier.

Reynaldo: Polonius' servant.
Players
Two gravediggers
Fortinbras: Prince of Norway.
A captain
English ambassadors
Gertrude: Queen of Denmark and mother of Hamlet.

Ophelia: Polonius' daughter.
Lords, ladies, officers, soldiers, sailors, messengers and **other attendants**
Ghost of Hamlet's father.

[Setting: Elsinore.]

ACT I

The gloomy setting of the first scene sets the tone of this dark drama of murder and revenge. It is midnight and bitterly cold as the guard is being changed on the battle platform of Elsinore Castle in Denmark. Francisco, the soldier on duty, is about to be relieved by his comrade, Bernardo, who is evidently anxious, for, instead of waiting in the darkness to be challenged, he nervously challenges Francisco:

> Who's there
> **Francisco:** Nay, answer me: stand, and unfold yourself.
> **Bernardo:** Long live the king!
> **Francisco:** Bernardo?
> **Bernardo:** He.
> **Francisco:** You come most carefully upon your hour.
> **Bernardo:** 'Tis now struck twelve; get thee to bed, Francisco.
> **Francisco:** For this relief much thanks: 'tis bitter cold,
> And I am sick at heart.
> **Bernardo:** Have you had quiet guard?
> **Francisco:** Not a mouse stirring.
> **Bernardo:** Well, good night.
> If you do meet Horatio and Marcellus,
> The rivals of my watch, bid them make haste.

The other two then appear. Marcellus and Bernardo, on the watch the two previous nights, had seen a dreadful apparition. Tonight, they have persuaded Horatio, a scholar, to watch with them so that "He may approve their eyes and speak to it."

Bernardo begins to tell Horatio what they have seen. Just at this time of night, "the bell then beating one," but his story is interrupted by the ghost's arrival. It looks like the late King Hamlet. When Horatio attempts to speak to it, it stalks away. They continue to comment upon the ghost's striking resemblance to the late king when he fought against Norway. The ghost had appeared twice before dressed like this. Horatio says:

In what particular thought to work I know not;
But, in the gross and scope of my opinion,
This bodes some strange eruption to our state.

Then Marcellus asks why the state has been recently disrupted by warlike preparations of all kinds. Horatio says it is probably due to rumors regarding an attempt to be made by young Fortinbras, prince of Norway, to regain lands lost by his father to King Hamlet in battle. It is because of this threat of war, Bernardo thinks, that King Hamlet's ghost has appeared. At this moment, the ghost reappears, and Horatio exclaims:

I'll cross it, though it blast me. Stay, illusion!
If thou hast any sound, or use of voice,
Speak to me:
If there be any good thing to be done,
That may to thee do ease and grace to me,
Speak to me:

Marcellus attempts to stop the ghost by striking it with his pike, but the spirit vanishes. "It was about to speak," notes Bernardo, "when the cock crew." Horatio adds that the ghost responded to the rooster's crow "like a guilty thing / Upon a fearful summons." Marcellus then offers an explanation for this phenomenon:

It faded on the crowing of the cock.
Some say that ever 'gainst that season comes
Wherein our Saviour's birth is celebrated,
The bird of dawning singeth all night long:
And then, they say, no spirit dare stir abroad,
The nights are wholesome, then no planets strike,
No fairy takes nor witch hath power to charm,
So hallow'd and so gracious is the time.

Horatio suggests that they tell young Hamlet about the ghost, which, though "dumb to us, will speak to him." Marcellus agrees, and the two of them go off in search of the prince.

The next morning, there is a gathering in the room of

state in the castle. The king and queen are there with Hamlet, Laertes and others, including Voltimand and Cornelius, prospective ambassadors to Norway. The king has on his mind his hurried marriage with his brother's widow and the threatened invasion by Fortinbras. Claudius begins by justifying his marriage:

> Though yet of Hamlet our dear brother's death
> The memory be green, and that it us befitted
> To bear our hearts in grief and our whole kingdom
> To be contracted in one brow of woe,
> Yet so far hath discretion fought with nature
> That we with wisest sorrow think on him,
> Together with remembrance of ourselves.
> Therefore our sometime sister, now our queen,
> The imperial jointress to this warlike state,
> Have we, as 'twere with a defeated joy,
> With an auspicious and a dropping eye,
> With mirth in funeral and with dirge in marriage,
> In equal scale weighing delight and dole,
> Taken to wife.

The king then reviews the threat of war presented by Fortinbras, but he dismisses this danger confidently: "So much for him." Claudius reveals how he has handled this young upstart:

> ... we have here writ
> To Norway, uncle of young Fortinbras,
> Who, impotent and bed-rid, scarcely hears
> Of this his nephew's purpose, — to suppress
> His further gait herein ...

Voltimand and Cornelius are sent to Norway to deliver the king's letter.

These matters settled, the king turns next to Laertes, who has requested permission to return to Paris, where he had come from to attend the coronation. When the king is assured by Polonius, Laertes' father, that he is willing to let the young man go, the king readily gives his consent. He now turns to Hamlet:

But now, my cousin Hamlet, and my son, —
Hamlet: *[Aside]* A little more than kin, and less than kind.
King: How is it that the clouds still hang on you?
Hamlet: Not so, my lord; I am too much i' the sun.
Queen: Good Hamlet, cast thy nighted colour off,
And let thine eye look like a friend on Denmark.
Do not for ever with thy veiled lids
Seek for thy noble father in the dust:
Thou know'st 'tis common; all that lives must die,
Passing through nature to eternity.
Hamlet: Ay, madam, it is common.
Queen: If it be,
Why seems it so particular with thee?
Hamlet: Seems, madam! nay, it is; I know not 'seems.'
'Tis not alone my inky cloak, good mother,
Nor customary suits of solemn black,
Nor windy suspiration of forced breath,
No, nor the fruitful river in the eye,
Nor the dejected haviour of the visage,
Together with all forms, moods, shapes of grief,
That can denote me truly: these indeed seem,
For they are actions that a man might play:
But I have that within which passeth show;
These but the trappings and the suits of woe.

Praising Hamlet for his loyalty to his father's memory, Claudius also tries to persuade his nephew that excessive grief is "a fault to heaven, / A fault against the dead, a fault to nature." The king and queen both try to cheer Hamlet and convince him to remain at Elsinore, rather than return to school in Wittenburg. Hamlet consents rather sullenly to this request. After the king and queen have left, Hamlet reveals his true feelings in an emotional soliloquy:

O, that this too too sullied flesh would melt,
Thaw and resolve itself into a dew!
Or that the Everlasting had not fix'd
His canon 'gainst self-slaughter! O God! God!
How weary, stale, flat and unprofitable

Seem to me all the uses of this world!
Fie on 't! ah fie! 'tis an unweeded garden,
That grows to seed; things rank and gross in nature
Possess it merely. That it should come to this!
But two months dead! nay, not so much, not two:
So excellent a king; that was, to this,
Hyperion to a satyr: so loving to my mother,
That he might not beteem the winds of heaven
Visit her face too roughly. Heaven and earth,
Must I remember? Why, she would hang on him
As if increase of appetite had grown
By what it fed on, and yet within a month
Let me not think on't; frailty thy name is woman

. . . .

O God, a beast that wants discourse of reason
Would have mourned longer — married with my
  uncle,
My father's brother, but no more like my father
Than I to Hercules.

. . . .

O, most wicked speed, to post
With such dexterity to incestuous sheets!
It is not nor it cannot come to good.
But break my heart, for I must hold my tongue.

Horatio enters with Marcellus and Bernardo. Hamlet greets them and he asks Horatio, his friend and fellow student in Wittenburg, what brings him to Elsinore. In answer to Horatio's explanation that he came to attend King Hamlet's funeral, young Hamlet replies:

I prithee do not mock me, fellow student.
I think it was to see my mother's wedding.

"The funeral baked meats / Did coldly furnish forth the marriage tables," Hamlet adds bitterly.

The conversation now turns to Hamlet's father. Horatio reveals the strange events he witnessed during the previous night's watch. Hamlet, shocked and excited by this news, questions Horatio extensively. Hamlet decides to join the others on the watch that night.

After all have left, Hamlet remarks:

My father's spirit in arms! all is not well;
I doubt some foul play: would the night were come!
Till then sit still, my soul: foul deeds will rise,
Though all the earth o'erwhelm them, to men's eyes.

In the home of Polonius, Laertes is saying good-bye to his sister, Ophelia. He asks her to write frequently and then he warns her against Prince Hamlet:

For Hamlet, and the trifling of his favour,
Hold it a fashion, and a toy in blood,
A violet in the youth of primy nature,
Forward, not permanent, sweet, not lasting,
The perfume and suppliance of a minute;
No more.
. . . .
The canker galls the infants of the spring
Too oft before their buttons be disclosed,
And in the morn and liquid dew of youth
Contagious blastments are most imminent.
Be wary then; best safety lies in fear:
Youth to itself rebels, though none else near.

Ophelia responds to her brother's advice about her maidenly conduct with some advice of her own:

I shall the effect of this good lesson keep,
As watchman to my heart. But, good my brother,
Do not, as some ungracious pastors do,
Show me the steep and thorny way to heaven,
Whilst, like a puff'd and reckless libertine,
Himself the primrose path of dalliance treads
And recks not his own rede.

This talk is interrupted by Polonius, who feels the need to hasten Laertes' departure and to give him some parting advice:

Look thou character. Give thy thoughts no tongue,

Nor any unproportion'd thought his act.
Be thou familiar, but by no means vulgar.
Those friends thou hast, and their adoption tried,
Grapple them to thy soul with hoops of steel,
But do not dull thy palm with entertainment
Of each new-hatch'd unfledged comrade. Beware
Of entrance to a quarrel; but being in,
Bear 't, that the opposed may beware of thee.
Give every man thy ear, but few thy voice:
Take each man's censure, but reserve thy
  judgement.
Costly thy habit as thy purse can buy,
But not express'd in fancy; rich, not gaudy:
For the apparel oft proclaims the man;
And they in France of the best rank and station
Are most select and generous chief in that.
Neither a borrower nor a lender be:
For loan oft loses both itself and friend,
And borrowing dulls the edge of husbandry.
This above all: to thine own self be true,
And it must follow, as the night the day,
Thou canst not then be false to any man.

As Laertes leaves, he again turns to Ophelia and asks her to remember what he had said to her. After he has gone, Polonius asks Ophelia what she and her brother had been discussing. "Something touching Lord Hamlet," she answers dutifully. She proceeds to explain, in response to further questioning, that Hamlet has "of late made many tenders/Of his affection to me." Polonius now offers his advice on how Ophelia should behave toward Hamlet:

Marry, I'll teach you: think yourself a baby,
That you have ta'en these tenders for true pay,
Which are not sterling. Tender yourself more dearly;
Or — not to crack the wind of the poor phrase.
Running it thus — you'll tender me a fool.

Although Ophelia protests that Hamlet has treated her in an honorable fashion, Polonius cynically cautions her:

From this time
Be something scanter of your maiden presence;
Set your entreatments at a higher rate
Than a command to parley. For Lord Hamlet,
Believe so much in him, that he is young,
And with a larger tether may he walk
Than may be given you: in few, Ophelia,
Do not believe his vows; for they are brokers,
Not of that dye which their investments show,
But mere implorators of unholy suits,
Breathing like sanctified and pious bawds,
The better to beguile. This is for all:
I would not, in plain terms, from this time forth,
Have you so slander any moment leisure,
As to give words or talk with the Lord Hamlet.
Look to 't, I charge you: come your ways.
Ophelia: I shall obey, my lord.

It is now just after midnight. Hamlet, Horatio and Marcellus are on the platform awaiting the appearance of the ghost. Trumpets and the firing of cannons are heard. While they are talking, the ghost appears, and Hamlet turns to speak to it:

Angels and ministers of grace defend us!
Be thou a spirit of health or goblin damn'd,
Bring with thee airs from heaven or blasts from hell
Be thy intents wicked or charitable,
Thou comest in such a questionable shape
That I will speak to thee: I'll call thee Hamlet,
King, father, royal Dane: O, answer me!

As the ghost motions to Hamlet, the others try to keep the prince from following, but Hamlet says:

Why, what should be the fear?
I do not set my life at a pin's fee;
And for my soul, what can it do to that,
Being a thing immortal as itself?
It waves me forth again: I'll follow it.

So Hamlet follows the ghost, and the others start to follow, in case some danger should come to him. Marcellus exclaims that "Something is rotten in the state of Denmark." The ghost only leads Hamlet to another part of the platform, and, when the prince demands to know what all this means, the ghost says:

I am thy father's spirit;
Doom'd for a certain term to walk the night,
And for the day confined to fast in fires,
Till the foul crimes done in my days of nature
Are burnt and purged away. But that I am forbid
To tell the secrets of my prison-house,
I could a tale unfold whose lightest word
Would harrow up thy soul, freeze thy young blood,
Make thy two eyes, like stars, start from their
spheres,
Thy knotted and combined locks to part
And each particular hair to stand an end,
Like quills upon the fretful porpentine:
But this eternal blazon must not be
To ears of flesh and blood. List, list, O, list!
If thou didst ever thy dear father love —
Hamlet: O God!
Ghost: Revenge his foul and most unnatural murder.
Hamlet: Murder!
Ghost: Murder most foul, as in the best it is,
But this most foul, strange, and unnatural.

The ghost reveals the true circumstances of the king's death. Although it is believed that King Hamlet was "stung by a serpent" (bitten by a snake) while sleeping in his orchard, he was, in fact, poisoned by Claudius, who poured a "leperous distilment" in the sleeping king's ear. Thus, the ghost continues, he was deprived "Of life, of crown, of queen" and even of the opportunity to confess his sins before death. The ghost now urges Hamlet to seek revenge:

If thou hast nature in thee, bear it not;
Let not the royal bed of Denmark be
A couch for luxury and damned incest.

Hamlet is not, however, to take action against his mother:

But, howsoever thou pursuest this act,
Taint not thy mind, nor let thy soul contrive
Against thy mother aught: leave her to heaven,
And to those thorns that in her bosom lodge,
To prick and sting her.

Morning is now approaching, and the ghost must return to purgatory. Alone, Hamlet rages aloud:

O all you host of heaven! O earth! what else?
And shall I couple hell? O, fie! Hold, hold, my heart;
And you, my sinews, grow not instant old,
But bear me stiffly up. Remember thee!
Ay, thou poor ghost, while memory holds a seat
In this distracted globe. Remember thee!
Yea, from the table of my memory
I'll wipe away all trivial fond records,
All saws of books, all forms, all pressures past,
That youth and observation copied there;
And thy commandment all alone shall live
Within the book and volume of my brain,
Unmix'd with baser matter: yes, by heaven!
O most pernicious woman!
O villain, villain, smiling, damned villain!

Then, Horatio and the others burst in full of questions, which Hamlet avoids answering as best as he can. Though confused by Hamlet's "wild and whirling words," they all swear upon the prince's sword that they will reveal nothing of what they have witnessed. They also agree not to give the slightest indication of knowing the reason for Hamlet's behavior if he should choose to pretend to be mentally deranged. As Hamlet and the rest are about to leave the platform, the prince remarks,

The time is out of joint: O cursed spite,
That ever I was born to set it right!

ACT II

By this time, Laertes has been in Paris long enough to run out of funds, and Polonius is sending more by his servant, Reynaldo. At the same time, Polonius is ordering Reynaldo to inquire in Paris what reputation Laertes has and how he has been behaving. The questioning, he says, should be carried out by slandering and criticizing Laertes. Polonius explains the reasoning behind this method of discovering how Laertes has behaved:

> Your bait of falsehood takes this carp of truth:
> And thus do we of wisdom and of reach,
> With windlasses and with assays of bias,
> By indirections find directions out:
> So, by my former lecture and advice,
> Shall you my son. You have me, have you not?

After Reynaldo leaves, Ophelia enters. Noticing that she seems upset, Polonius questions her and receives the following reply:

> My lord, as I was sewing in my closet,
> Lord Hamlet, with his doublet all unbraced,
> No hat upon his head, his stockings foul'd,
> Ungarter'd and down-gyved to his ancle;
> Pale as his shirt, his knees knocking each other,
> And with a look so piteous in purport
> As if he had been loosed out of hell
> To speak of horrors, he comes before me.

"Mad for thy love?" Polonius asks. Then he demands to know more of what took place between Hamlet and Ophelia. She obediently provides her father with an account of how Hamlet took her hand and stared at her face "As he would draw it," "raised a sigh so piteous and profound / As it did seem to shatter all his bulk" and left the room "with his head over his shoulder turn'd." Polonius decides that they must tell the king immediately about Hamlet's strange appearance and behavior. The lord chamberlain believes that the prince has been driven mad by Ophelia's rejecting him, according to her father's wishes.

In the castle, meanwhile, the king and queen are welcoming two young men, Rosencrantz and Guildenstern, old friends of Hamlet. They have been sent for in the hope that they will be able to discover the cause for the change in Hamlet during the last few weeks. As the two go out to find Hamlet, Polonius enters in considerable excitement. He thinks he has discovered the cause of what he calls Hamlet's madness. The king is eager to hear, but first he has to listen as the ambassadors to Norway report that the king of Norway has forbidden Fortinbras' original expedition, but begs the consent of Claudius to let Fortinbras march across Denmark to attack the Poles. The king consents to this and dismisses the ambassadors with thanks. Then Polonius breaks out impatiently:

This business is well ended.
My liege, and madam, to expostulate
What majesty should be, what duty is,
Why day is day, night night, and time is time,
Were nothing but to waste night, day and time.
Therefore, since brevity is the soul of wit
And tediousness the limbs and outward flourishes,
I will be brief. Your noble son is mad:
Mad call I it; for, to define true madness,
What is 't but to be nothing else but mad?
But let that go.
Queen: More matter, with less art.
Polonius: Madam, I swear I use no art at all.
That he is mad, 'tis true: 'tis true 'tis pity,
And pity 'tis 'tis true: a foolish figure;
But farewell it, for I will use no art.
Mad let us grant him then: and now remains
That we find out the cause of this effect,
Or rather say, the cause of this defect,
For this effect defective comes by cause:
Thus it remains and the remainder thus.
Perpend.
I have a daughter, — have while she is mine, —
Who in her duty and obedience, mark,
Hath given me this: now gather and surmise.

Polonius, with frequent self-interruptions and irrelevant comments, finally reads a love letter written by Hamlet to Ophelia. He then offers his theory of what lies behind Hamlet's madness:

> . . . I prescripts gave [Ophelia]
> That she should lock herself from [Hamlet's] resort,
> Admit no messengers, receive no tokens.
> Which done, she took the fruits of my advice;
> And he repulsed, a short tale to make,
> Fell into a sadness, then into a fast,
> Thence to a watch, thence into a weakness,
> Thence to a lightness, and by this declension
> Into the madness wherein now he raves
> And all we mourn for.

The king and queen seem to accept Polonius' opinion on the matter of Hamlet's madness. They also agree with the lord chamberlain's plan to test this theory:

> . . . I'll loose my daughter to him:
> Be you and I behind an arras then;
> Mark the encounter: if he loves her not,
> And be not from his reason fall'n thereon,
> Let me be no assistant for a state,
> But keep a farm and carters.

Hamlet now enters, reading. Polonius starts to speak to the prince, and a confused conversation follows:

> **Polonius:** O, give me leave: how does my good Lord Hamlet?
> **Hamlet:** Well, God-a-mercy.
> **Polonius:** Do you know me, my lord?
> **Hamlet:** Excellent well; you are a fishmonger.
> **Polonius:** Not I, my lord.
> **Hamlet:** Then I would you were so honest a man.
> **Polonius:** Honest, my lord!
> **Hamlet:** Ay, sir; to be honest, as this world goes, is to be one man picked out of ten thousand.
> **Polonius:** That's very true, my lord.

Hamlet: For if the sun breed maggots in a dead dog, being a god kissing carrion — Have you a daughter?
Polonius: I have, my lord.
Hamlet: Let her not walk i' the sun: conception is a blessing; but not as your daughter may conceive, — friend, look to 't.
Polonius: *[Aside.]* How say you by that? Still harping on my daughter: yet he knew me not at first; he said I was a fishmonger: he is far gone: and truly in my youth I suffered much extremity for love; very near this. I'll speak to him again. — What do you read, my lord?
Hamlet: Words, words, words.
Polonius: What is the matter, my lord?
Hamlet: Between who?
Polonius: I mean, the matter that you read, my lord.
Hamlet: Slanders, sir: for the satirical rogue says here that old men have grey beards, that their faces are wrinkled, their eyes purging thick amber and plum-tree gum, and that they have a plentiful lack of wit, together with most weak hams: all which, sir, though I most powerfully and potently believe, yet I hold it not honesty to have it thus set down; for yourself, sir, should be old as I am, if like a crab you could go backward.
Polonius: *[Aside.]* Though this be madness, yet there is method in 't.

Polonius, deciding that he must "contrive the means of meeting between [Hamlet] and [his] daughter," leaves the prince.

Rosencrantz and Guildenstern come seeking Hamlet. He welcomes them eagerly, and the conversation turns to the unpredictability of fortunes and how outward things are colored by men's thoughts. Hamlet eventually asks what brings these two to Elsinore:

> Were you not sent for? Is it your own inclining? Is it a free visitation? Come, deal justly with me: come, come; nay, speak.

Rosencrantz and Guildenstern admit, finally, that they have been summoned by the king and queen, and Hamlet proceeds to tell them why so that his guessing will spare them from having to report back that they gave themselves away:

> I have of late — but wherefore I know not — lost all my mirth, forgone all custom and exercises; and indeed it goes so heavily with my disposition that this goodly frame, the earth, seems to me a sterile promontory; this most excellent canopy, the air, look you, this brave o'erhanging firmament, this majestical roof fretted with golden fire, why, it appears no other thing to me than a foul and pestilent congregation of vapours. What a piece of work is a man! how noble in reason! how infinite in faculty! in form and moving how express and admirable! in action how like an angel! in apprehension how like a god! the beauty of the world! the paragon of animals! and yet, to me, what is this quintessence of dust? man delights not me; no, nor woman neither, though by your smiling you seem to say so.

Then the two tell Hamlet of a company of players that they passed on the way. When Hamlet asks why the players were on the road, Rosencrantz says it was because companies of child players had become so popular in the city that the professionals had no audiences. At this moment, the players are announced, and Hamlet dismisses the two friends with these words:

> Gentlemen, you are welcome to Elsinore. Your hands, come then: the appurtenance of welcome is fashion and ceremony: let me comply with you in this garb, lest my extent to the players, which, I tell you, must show fairly outwards, should more appear like entertainment than yours. You are welcome: but my uncle-father and aunt-mother are deceived.
> **Guildenstern:** In what, my dear Lord?
> **Hamlet:** I am but mad north-north-west: when the wind is southerly I know a hawk from a handsaw.

Polonius comes to announce the players, whom he highly recommends:

> The best actors in the world, either for tragedy, comedy, history, pastoral, pastoral-comical, historical-pastoral, tragical-historical, tragical-comical-historical-pastoral, scene individable, or poem unlimited: Seneca cannot be too heavy, nor Plautus too light. For the law of writ and the liberty, these are the only men.

When the players enter, Polonius greets them warmly and he asks one of them to recite "a passionate speech." Hamlet asks that the player offer his version of Aeneas' tale to Dido, in which he describes Priam's slaughter. Hamlet begins the speech, and, after a few lines, the players take over. It is about the destruction of Troy and the killing of Priam by Pyrrhus, a tragedy mourned by Hecuba. When the speech is finished, Hamlet turns the players over to Polonius. Polonius and all the players, except the first, leave. Alone with this player, Hamlet makes a request:

> Dost thou hear me, old friend; can you play *The Murder of Gonzago*?
> **First Player:** Ay, my lord.
> **Hamlet:** We'll ha 't to-morrow night. You could, for a need, study a speech of some dozen or sixteen lines, which I would set down and insert in 't, could you not?
> **First Player:** Ay, my lord.

When all are gone, Hamlet, by himself, thinks over the actor's speech:

> Now I am alone.
> O, what a rogue and peasant slave am I!
> Is it not monstrous that this player here,
> But in a fiction, in a dream of passion,
> Could force his soul so to his own conceit
> That from her working all his visage wann'd;
> Tears in his eyes, distraction in 's aspect,

A broken voice, and his whole function suiting
With forms to his conceit? and all for nothing!
For Hecuba!
What's Hecuba to him, or he to Hecuba,
That he should weep for her? What would he do,
Had he the motive and the cue for passion
That I have? He would drown the stage with tears
And cleave the general ear with horrid speech,
Make mad the guilty and appal the free,
Confound the ignorant, and amaze indeed
The very faculties of eyes and ears.
Yet I,
A dull and muddy-mettled rascal, peak,
Like John-a-dreams, unpregnant of my cause,
And can say nothing; no, not for a king,
Upon whose property and most dear life
A damn'd defeat was made. Am I a coward?
Who calls me villain? breaks my pate across?
Plucks off my beard, and blows it in my face?
Tweaks me by the nose? gives me the lie i' the
  throat,
As deep as to the lungs? who does me this?
Ha!
'Swounds, I should take it: for it cannot be
But I am pigeon-liver'd and lack gall
To make oppression bitter, or ere this
I should have fatted all the region kites
With this slave's offal: bloody, bawdy villain!
Remorseless, treacherous, lecherous, kindless
  villain!
O, vengeance!
Why, what an ass am I! This is most brave,
That I, the son of a dear father murder'd,
Prompted to my revenge by heaven and hell,
Must, like a whore, unpack my heart with words,
And fall a-cursing, like a very drab,
A scullion!
Fie upon 't! foh! About, my brain! Hum, I have
  heard
That guilty creatures, sitting at a play,
Have by the very cunning of the scene

Been struck so to the soul that presently
They have proclaim'd their malefactions;
For murder, though it have no tongue, will speak
With most miraculous organ. I'll have these players
Play something like the murder of my father
Before mine uncle: I'll observe his looks;
I'll tent him to the quick: if he but blench,
I know my course. The spirit that I have seen
May be the devil; and the devil hath power
To assume a pleasing shape; yea, and perhaps
Out of my weakness and my melancholy,
As he is very potent with such spirits,
Abuses me to damn me. I'll have grounds
More relative than this. The play's the thing
Wherein I'll catch the conscience of the king.

ACT III

Rosencrantz and Guildenstern are now telling the king, the queen and Ophelia about the interview they have just had with Hamlet. They confess that they could not make him reveal his true condition, but that he seemed pleased to greet certain players and he asked them to present a play before the court that night. The king sends the two young men back to Hamlet, then turns to the queen with these words:

Sweet Gertrude, leave us too;
For we have closely sent for Hamlet hither,
That he, as 'twere by accident, may here
Affront Ophelia:
Her father and myself, lawful espials,
Will so bestow ourselves that, seeing unseen,
We may of their encounter frankly judge,
And gather by him, as he is behaved,
If 't be the affliction of his love or no
That thus he suffers for.

Before the queen leaves, she turns to Ophelia and expresses the hope that the young woman's "good beauties be the happy cause / Of Hamlet's wildness" and that her virtues may now restore him to his former ways. Polonius instructs Ophelia to sit and read a book so that

show of such an exercise may colour
Your loneliness. We are oft to blame in this,
'Tis too much proved — that with devotion's visage
And pious action we do sugar o'er
The devil himself.

Hearing these words, the king guiltily remarks:

[Aside] O, 'tis too true!
How smart a lash that speech doth give my
conscience!
The harlot's cheek, beautied with plastering art,
Is not more ugly to the thing that helps it
Than is my deed to my most painted word:
O heavy burthen!

Polonius and the king conceal themselves, according to plan.

Hamlet now enters and utters his most famous soliloquy:

To be, or not to be: that is the question:
Whether 'tis nobler in the mind to suffer
The slings and arrows of outrageous fortune,
Or to take arms against a sea of troubles,
And by opposing end them. To die: to sleep;
No more; and by a sleep to say we end
The heart-ache, and the thousand natural shocks
That flesh is heir to, 'tis a consummation
Devoutly to be wish'd. To die, to sleep;
To sleep: perchance to dream: ay, there's the rub;
For in that sleep of death what dreams may come,
When we have shuffled off this mortal coil,
Must give us pause: there's the respect
That makes calamity of so long life;
For who would bear the whips and scorns of time,
The oppressor's wrong, the proud man's contumely,
The pangs of despised love, the law's delay,
The insolence of office, and the spurns
That patient merit of the unworthy takes,
When he himself might his quietus make
With a bare bodkin? who would fardels bear,
To grunt and sweat under a weary life,
But that the dread of something about death,
The undiscover'd country from whose bourn
No traveller returns, puzzles the will,
And makes us rather bear those ills we have
Than fly to others that we know not of?
Thus conscience does make cowards of us all,
And thus the native hue of resolution
Is sicklied o'er with the pale cast of thought,
And enterprises of great pith and moment
With this regard their currents turn awry
And lose the name of action.

Hamlet suddenly notices Ophelia and greets her graciously. Ophelia offers to return to Hamlet "remembrances" that he had given her, but the prince denies ever having given her anything. Ophelia protests, and Hamlet begins to question her honesty and beauty in an abrupt and aggressive manner. Hamlet next tells Ophelia that he loved her once, then that he loved her not at all. Finally, Hamlet dismisses Ophelia altogether:

> Get thee to a nunnery: why wouldst thou be a breeder of sinners? I am myself indifferent honest; but yet I could accuse me of such things that it were better my mother had not borne me: I am very proud, revengeful, ambitious; with more offences at my beck than I have thoughts to put them in, imagination to give them shape, or time to act them in. What should such fellows as I do crawling between heaven and earth? We are arrant knaves all; believe none of us. Go thy ways to a nunnery.

Hamlet, as though suspecting Polonius' presence, asks, "Where's your father?" When Ophelia replies that he is at home, Hamlet declares, "Let the doors be shut upon him, that he may play the fool no where but in's own house." Hamlet then returns to his condemnation of Ophelia:

> If thou dost marry, I'll give thee this plague for thy dowry: be thou as chaste as ice, as pure as snow, thou shalt not escape calumny. Get thee to a nunnery, go: farewell. Or, if thou wilt needs marry, marry a fool; for wise men know well enough what monsters you make of them. To a nunnery, go; and quickly too. Farewell.

Ophelia mourns the madness that has possessed Hamlet and toppled him from the heights of greatness:

> O, what a noble mind is here o'erthrown!
> The courtier's, soldier's, scholar's, eye, tongue,
>   sword:
> The expectancy and rose of the fair state,
> The glass of fashion and the mould of form,
> The observed of all observers, quite, quite down!
> And I, of ladies most deject and wretched,
> That suck'd the honey of his music vows,

Now see that noble and most sovereign reason,
Like sweet bells jangled, out of tune and harsh;
That unmatch'd form and feature of blown youth
Blasted with ecstasy: O, woe is me,
To have seen what I have seen, see what I see!

The king and Polonius now appear from their eavesdropping. The king does not think love is the cause of Hamlet's madness, nor does he think Hamlet speaks like a mad person:

There's something in his soul
O'er which his melancholy sits on brood,
And I do doubt the hatch and the disclose
Will be some danger.

Claudius decides that Hamlet represents a threat that must be disposed of. Therefore, he resolves to send Hamlet to England, in the hope that "the seas and countries different / ... shall expel / This something-settled matter in his heart." Polonius, who still believes Hamlet to be the victim of disappointment in love, suggests further eavesdropping:

Let his queen mother all alone entreat him
To show his grief: let her be round with him;
And I'll be placed, so please you, in the ear
Of all their conference. If she find him not,
To England send him, or confine him where
Your wisdom best shall think.
King: It shall be so:
Madness in great ones must not unwatch'd go.

That same evening, Hamlet is talking to the players before they give their performance. He is giving them a parting word of advice about their acting.

O, it offends me to the soul to hear a robustious periwig-pated fellow tear a passion to tatters, to very rags, to split the ears of the groundlings, who, for the most part, are capable of nothing but inexplicable dumb-shows and noise: I would have such a fellow whipped for o'erdoing. Termagant; it out-herods

Herod: pray you, avoid it.

When Polonius, Rosencrantz and Guildenstern enter, Hamlet asks whether the king and queen will attend the play, and he sends all three to summon the players. He then calls for Horatio. When Horatio comes in, Hamlet says:

Horatio, thou art e'en as just a man
As e'er my conversation coped withal.

Hamlet then proceeds to praise Horatio for having the very virtues that Hamlet himself lacks. Horatio is:

A man that fortune's buffets and rewards
Hast ta'en with equal thanks: and blest are those
Whose blood and judgement are so well commingle
That they are not a pipe for fortune's finger
To sound what stop she please. Give me that man
That is not passion's slave, and I will wear him
In my heart's core, ay, in my heart of heart,
As I do thee.

Having explained to Horatio why he respects his judgment so highly, Hamlet enlists his friend in his plan to observe Claudius during the performance of the play and determine if the king's reaction to several passages Hamlet has inserted in it reveals his guilt for the murder of his brother. Hamlet hopes thus to test the ghost's accusation of Claudius.

With a Danish march and a flourish of trumpets, the king, the queen, Polonius, Ophelia and courtiers come to view the play. After some conversation among them all, Hamlet sits down at Ophelia's feet and speaks to her in a tone that she calls merry. The first part of the performance, a dumb show, is presented:

A king *and a* queen *enter very lovingly; the* queen *embracing him, and he her. She kneels, and makes show of protestation unto him. He takes her up, and declines his head upon her neck: lays him down upon a bank of flowers: she, seeing him asleep, leaves him. Anon comes in a fellow, takes off his crown, kisses it, and pours poison in the* king's *ears, and exits. The* queen *returns; finds the* king *dead, and makes passionate action. The poisoner, with some two or three* mutes, *comes in again, seeming to lament with her. The dead body is carried away. The poisoner wooes the* queen *with gifts: she seems loath and unwilling awhile, but in the end accepts his love.*

The Murder of Gonzago is now presented. The action in the play is similar to that of the dumb show, up to the point where the murderer, identified as Lucianus, the king's nephew, pours poison in the king's ear. The player-queen insists that she will never remarry should she become a widow. Hamlet now takes the opportunity to ask his mother how she likes the play. "The lady doth protest too much," she answers. Claudius then inquires about the name of the play, and Hamlet tells him it is called "The Mouse-trap." The prince becomes more excited as the play nears its climax. When the murderer pours the poison into the player-king's ear, he assures the audience that they will soon see how the murderer "gets the love of Gonzago's wife." Alarmed, Claudius rises, calling "Give me some light. Away!" Hamlet is delighted at the king's reaction, for he feels it proves his guilt.

In this moment of triumph, Rosencrantz and Guildenstern come to report that the king has retired to his chamber in great anger and that the queen wishes to see her son.

Hamlet's ironic remarks reveal his contempt for these so-called friends. He asks Guildenstern to play one of the actor's recorders and, when Guildenstern protests that he does not know how, Hamlet angrily remarks:

> Why, look you now, how unworthy a thing you make of me! You would play upon me; you would seem to know my stops; you would pluck out the heart of my mystery; you would sound me from my lowest note to the top of my compass: and there is much music, excellent voice, in this little organ; yet cannot you make it speak. 'Sblood, do you think I am easier to be played on than a pipe? Call me what instrument you will, though you can fret me, you cannot play upon me.

Polonius enters and repeats the request that Hamlet go to see his mother in her chamber. Hamlet, agreeing that he will be there "by and by," dismisses everyone and speaks in soliloquy:

'Tis now the very witching time of night,
When churchyards yawn, and hell itself breathes out
Contagion to this world: now could I drink hot blood,
And do such bitter business as the day
Would quake to look on. Soft! now to my mother.
O heart, lose not thy nature; let not ever
The soul of Nero enter this firm bosom:
Let me be cruel, not unnatural:
I will speak daggers to her, but use none;
My tongue and soul in this be hypocrites;
How in my words soever she be shent,
To give them seals never, my soul, consent!

Rosencrantz and Guildenstern have gone back to the king's chamber. Claudius tells them that he is sending them to England with Hamlet, who must be removed at once from Denmark for the good of the realm. Rosencrantz supports this view:

The single and peculiar life is bound
With all the strength and armour of the mind
To keep itself from noyance; but much more
That spirit upon whose weal depends and rests
The lives of many. The cease of majesty
Dies not alone, but like a gulf doth draw
What's near it with it: it is a massy wheel,
Fix'd on the summit of the highest mount,
To whose huge spokes ten thousand lesser things
Are mortised and adjoin'd; which, when it falls,
Each small annexment, petty consequence,
Attends the boisterous ruin. Never alone
Did the king sigh, but with a general groan.

As the king sends them out to prepare for the voyage, Polonius comes to report Hamlet's movements. Polonius offers to conceal himself behind the tapestry in the queen's chamber to spy on the conversation between mother and son. The king thanks the lord chamberlain for this service.

After Polonius leaves, Claudius, in a soliloquy, expresses his feelings of guilt and his inability to atone for his sins through prayer:

> O, my offence is rank, it smells to heaven;
> It hath the primal eldest curse upon 't,
> A brother's murder. Pray can I not,
> Though inclination be as sharp as will:
> My stronger guilt defeats my strong intent,
> And like a man to double business bound,
> I stand in pause where I shall first begin,
> And both neglect. What if this cursed hand
> Were thicker than itself with brother's blood,
> Is there not rain enough in the sweet heavens
> To wash it white as snow? Whereto serves mercy
> But to confront the visage of offence?
> And what's in prayer but this twofold force,
> To be forestalled ere we come to fall,
> Or pardon'd being down? Then I'll look up;
> My fault is past. But O, what form of prayer
> Can serve my turn? 'Forgive me my foul murder?'
> That cannot be, since I am still possess'd
> Of those effects for which I did the murder,
> My crown, mine own ambition and my queen.
> May one be pardon'd and retain the offence?
> In the corrupted currents of this world
> Offence's gilded hand may shove by justice,
> And oft 'tis seen the wicked prize itself
> Buys out the law: but 'tis not so above;
> There is no shuffling, there the action lies
> In his true nature, and we ourselves compell'd
> Even to the teeth and forehead of our faults
> To give in evidence. What then? what rests?
> Try what repentance can: what can it not?
> Yet what can it when one can not repent?
> O wretched state! O bosom black as death!
> O limed soul, that struggling to be free
> Art more engaged! Help, angels! make assay!
> Bow, stubborn knees, and, heart with strings of steel,

Be soft as sinews of the new-born babe!
All may be well.

Hamlet enters quietly. Seeing Claudius at prayer, he decides that this may be the perfect opportunity to avenge the murder of his father. But another idea suddenly occurs to Hamlet: if he kills Claudius while he is praying, the villain will go to heaven, all his sins being confessed. Hamlet's father, though, had no opportunity to confess himself before he was murdered. With this in mind, Hamlet declares,

No.
Up, sword, and know thou a more horrid hent:
When he is drunk asleep, or in his rage,
Or in the incestuous pleasure of his bed;
At gaming, swearing, or about some act
That has no relish of salvation in 't;
Then trip him, that his heels may kick at heaven
And that his soul may be as damn'd and black
As hell, whereto it goes. My mother stays:
This physic but prolongs thy sickly days.

Ironically, though, the king's prayer offers him no comfort.

My words fly up, my thoughts remain below:
Words without thoughts never to heaven go.

Meanwhile, Polonius has gone to the queen's chamber. As he is telling her that Hamlet will come immediately, they hear him calling her. Before Hamlet comes in, Polonius dodges behind the hangings in the room. Hamlet enters and begins to speak to his mother in an insulting manner. Frightened by Hamlet's angry remarks and threatening tone, Gertrude cries out for help. Polonius, behind the hangings, echoes her cry. Hamlet exclaims, "How now! a rat? Dead, for a ducat, dead." He thrusts his sword through the hangings, killing the lord chamberlain. Gertrude regrets this "rash and bloody deed," but Hamlet excitedly points out,

A bloody deed! almost as bad, good mother.
As kill a king, and marry with his brother.

Hamlet then speaks a few unfeeling words of farewell over the body of Polonius:

Thou wretched, rash, intruding fool, farewell!
I took thee for thy better: take thy fortune;
Thou find'st to be too busy in some danger.
Leave wringing of your hands: peace! sit you down,
And let me wring your heart: for so I shall,
If it be made of penetrable stuff;
If damned custom have not brass'd it so,
That it be proof and bulwark against sense.

Hamlet turns to his mother and accuses her of having committed

Such an act
That blurs the grace and blush of modesty,
Calls virtue hypocrite, takes off the rose
From the fair forehead of an innocent love,
And sets a blister there; makes marriage vows
As false as dicers' oaths: O, such a deed
As from the body of contraction plucks
The very soul, and sweet religion makes
A rhapsody of words: heaven's face doth glow;
Yea, this solidity and compound mass,
With tristful visage, as against the doom,
Is thought-sick at the act.

Hamlet shows Gertrude a picture of her late husband and one of Claudius. He compares the grace and nobility of the former with the unwholesomeness of the latter. He then wonders how her judgment could have been so flawed that she abandoned the memory of her first husband to marry an inferior man such as Claudius. Stung by Hamlet's words, the queen begs him to stop, but he persists in tormenting her:

Queen: O Hamlet, speak no more:
Thou turn'st mine eyes into my very soul,
And there I see such black and grained spots
As will not leave their tinct.

Hamlet: Nay, but to live
In the rank sweat of an enseamed bed,
Stew'd in corruption, honeying and making love
Over the nasty sty, —
Queen: O, speak to me no more;
These words like daggers enter in my ears;
No more, sweet Hamlet!
Hamlet: A murderer and a villain;
A slave that is not twentieth part the tithe
Of your precedent lord; a vice of kings;
A cutpurse of the empire and the rule,
That from a shelf the precious diadem stole
And put it in his pocket!

Hamlet is interrupted by the appearance of the ghost, invisible to his mother. The ghost reminds Hamlet of his "almost blunted purpose," warning against undue harshness to Gertrude. The queen, thinking that Hamlet "bend[s] [his] eye on vacancy," takes Hamlet's conversation with the ghost to be a further indication of her son's madness.

Now softened toward his mother, Hamlet begs her to "Repent what's past, avoid what is to come." He asks her not to sleep with Claudius that night, to "Assume a virtue if you have it not." Refrain tonight, he continues, and it will be easier for her, in time, to stay away from the king's bed altogether. Gertrude assures Hamlet that she will not reveal what Hamlet has said to her. Hamlet reminds her, then, that he must leave for England. He tells her, too, that he does not trust Rosencrantz and Guildenstern, who are to accompany him on his journey:

There's letters seal'd: and my two schoolfellows,
Whom I will trust as I will adders fang'd,
They bear the mandate; they must sweep my way,
And marshal me to knavery. Let it work;
For 'tis the sport to have the engineer
Hoist with his own petar: and 't shall go hard
But I will delve one yard below their mines,
And blow them at the moon: O, 'tis most sweet
When in one line two crafts directly meet.

Remembering Polonius' body, Hamlet coldly announces that he will "lug the guts into the neighbouring room" and he says goodnight to his mother.

ACT IV

The queen tells the king that Hamlet is, without doubt, insane and, in his madness, has killed Polonius. The king realizes that he will be held more or less to blame for the death of Polonius, in that he did not have Hamlet restrained. Claudius is confirmed in his intent to send Hamlet to England. The queen says Hamlet has gone to remove the body of Polonius. When Rosencrantz and Guildenstern return, the king sends them to find Hamlet.

In another room in the castle, Hamlet is met by the two young men, who ask him where he has left the body of Polonius. Hamlet answers indirectly. Hamlet then calls Rosencrantz a sponge that "Soaks up the king's countenance, his rewards, his authorities." Unable to learn anything from Hamlet, Rosencrantz and Guildenstern leave.

As they go out, the king comes in, still determined to get Hamlet out of the way:

> I have sent to seek him, and to find the body.
> How dangerous is it that this man goes loose!
> Yet must not we put the strong law on him:
> He's loved of the distracted multitude,
> Who like not in their judgement, but their eyes;
> And where 'tis so, the offender's scourge is weigh'd,
> But never the offence. To bear all smooth and even,
> This sudden sending him away must seem
> Deliberate pause: diseases desperate grown
> By desperate appliance are relieved,
> Or not at all.

The king attempts to learn from Hamlet the whereabouts of the body, but Hamlet proves unco-operative again:

> **King:** Now, Hamlet, where's Polonius?
> **Hamlet:** At supper.
> **King:** At supper! where?
> **Hamlet:** Not where he eats, but where he is eaten: a certain convocation of politic worms are e'en at him. Your worm is your only emperor for diet: we fat all creatures else to fat us, and we fat ourselves for maggots: your fat king and your lean beggar is but

variable service, two dishes, but to one table: that's the end.
King: Alas, alas!
Hamlet: A man may fish with the worm that hath eat of a king, and eat of the fish that hath fed of that worm.
King: What dost thou mean by this?
Hamlet: Nothing but to show you how a king may go a progress through the guts of a beggar.
King: Where is Polonius?
Hamlet: In heaven; send thither to see: if your messenger find him not there, seek him i' the other place yourself. But indeed, if you find him not within this month, you shall nose him as you go up the stairs into the lobby.
King: Go seek him there.
[To some attendants.]
Hamlet: He will stay till you come.

At this point, the king tells Hamlet that the prince must leave for England immediately. As Hamlet goes out, the king sends Rosencrantz and Guildenstern to hasten the prince's departure. Then, Claudius reveals the full extent of his schemes:

And, England, if my love thou hold'st at aught
As my great power thereof may give thee sense,
Since yet thy cicatrice looks raw and red
After the Danish sword, and thy free awe
Pays homage to us — thou mayst not coldly set
Our sovereign process; which imports at full,
By letters congruing to that effect,
The present death of Hamlet. Do it, England;
For like the hectic in my blood he rages,
And thou must cure me: till I know 'tis done,
Howe'er my haps, my joys were ne'er begun.

While these events are going on, Fortinbras is leading his army across a plain in Denmark. He sends a captain to report his passage to the king. Just then, Hamlet and his two attendants appear on the way to their ship. Hamlet asks the captain the meaning of this expedition. The captain replies that they are on a mission "to gain a little patch of ground / That hath in it no profit but the name." Hamlet sends Rosencrantz and Guildenstern ahead, while he stays behind to review his own situation and compare it with that of Fortinbras:

How all occasions do inform against me,
And spur my dull revenge! What is a man,
If his chief good and market of his time
Be but to sleep and feed? a beast, no more.
Sure, he that made us with such large discourse,
Looking before and after, gave us not
That capability and god-like reason
To fust in us unused. Now, whether it be
Bestial oblivion, or some craven scruple
Of thinking too precisely on the event,
A thought which, quarter'd, hath but one part
wisdom
And ever three parts coward, — I do not know
Why yet I live to say 'this thing's to do,'
Sith I have cause, and will, and strength, and means,
To do 't. Examples gross as earth exhort me:
Witness this army, of such mass and charge,
Led by a delicate and tender prince,
Whose spirit with divine ambition puff'd
Makes mouths at the invisible event,
Exposing what is mortal and unsure
To all that fortune, death and danger dare,
Even for an egg-shell. Rightly to be great
Is not to stir without great argument,
But greatly to find quarrel in a straw
When honour's at the stake. How stand I then,
That have a father kill'd, a mother stain'd,
Excitements of my reason and my blood
And let all sleep, while to my shame I see
The imminent death of twenty thousand men,
That for a fantasy and trick of fame
Go to their graves like beds, fight for a plot
Whereon the numbers cannot try the cause,
Which is not tomb enough and continent

To hide the slain? O, from this time forth,
My thoughts be bloody, or be nothing worth!

In the castle, the queen, Horatio and a gentleman are talking about Ophelia, who wishes to speak to the queen. When the queen refuses to see her, the gentleman says that Ophelia "speaks things in doubt, / That carry but half sense." Horatio fears that "she may strew / Dangerous conjectures in ill-breeding minds" regarding Hamlet's part in Polonius' death. The queen, therefore, consents to see the disturbed young woman, who enters singing ballads thematically related to the death of her father and the seduction of an innocent maiden.

Claudius joins the group. He addresses Ophelia kindly, but he receives no rational reply. He is convinced that Polonius' death has driven Ophelia mad. He orders that she be closely watched. Claudius then reveals that Laertes, just returned from France, has been upset by rumors about the circumstances of his father's death.

Loud noises are heard, and a gentleman comes to tell the queen that the commotion is made by a crowd coming with Laertes, who is determined to demand vengeance for the death of his father. The people are crying out for Laertes to be king. Laertes comes in, armed and, after ordering his followers to stay outside, turns to the king and exclaims, "Give me my father!" The king and queen attempt to calm Laertes and explain the death of Polonius. Claudius succeeds in reasoning with him:

Why, now you speak
Like a good child and a true gentleman.
That I am guiltless of your father's death,
And am most sensibly in grief for it,
It shall as level to your judgement pierce
As day does to your eye.

Ophelia enters now, and Laertes has another cause for grief as he witnesses her strange behavior:

O heat, dry up my brains! tears seven times salt,
Burn out the sense and virtue of mine eye!

By heaven, thy madness shall be paid with weight,
Till our scale turn the beam. O rose of May!
Dear maid, kind sister, sweet Ophelia!
O heavens! is 't possible a young man's wits
Should be as mortal as an old man's life?
Nature is fine in love, and where 'tis fine
It sends some precious instance of itself
After the thing it loves.

Ophelia, still singing, distributes imaginary flowers to those present:

There's rosemary, that's for remembrance: pray you, love remember: and there is pansies, that's for thoughts.

When Ophelia leaves, the king promises to join Laertes in punishing the guilty in the matter of Polonius' death: "Where the offence is let the great axe fall."

In another room, Horatio appears with a servant, who tells him that some sailors wish to speak to him. When he meets them, one hands him a letter from Hamlet. Hamlet writes that his ship was attacked by pirates, who have brought him back to Denmark. The sailors also have letters for the king.

Meanwhile, the king and Laertes are discussing the death of Polonius. The king is explaining why he could not restrain Hamlet: the queen is greatly attached to him, and the common people love him. Laertes exclaims:

And so have I a noble father lost;
A sister driven into desperate terms,
Whose worth, if praises may go back again,
Stood challenger on mount of all the age
For her prefections: but my revenge will come.

The king tells him that he will soon hear what measures have been taken against Hamlet. At this moment, a messenger brings Hamlet's letter, revealing that he has returned to Denmark. The king, greatly surprised, realizes that something must be done at once to protect himself. He resolves to make use of Laertes' desire for revenge. He tells Laertes that Hamlet has heard how skilful a fencer Laertes is, and that the prince has been practising in hopes of matching skills with him. When the bout is at its fiercest, Laertes can substitute an unfoiled rapier and kill Hamlet. This plan pleases Laertes, and he proposes, to make Hamlet's death certain, to tip that rapier with a deadly poison. In addition, the king says, he will prepare a poison drink for Hamlet to take when he becomes hot and thirsty during the contest.

Just as this scheme has been arranged, the queen appears and announces the death of Ophelia. The queen offers a touching, poetic description of the maiden's death:

> There is a willow grows aslant a brook,
> That shows his hoar leaves in the glassy stream,
> There with fantastic garlands did she come
> Of crow-flowers, nettles, daisies, and long purples,
> That liberal shepherds give a grosser name,
> But our cold maids do dead men's fingers call them:
> There, on the pendent boughs her coronet weeds
> Clambering to hang, an envious sliver broke;
> When down her weedy trophies and herself
> Fell in the weeping brook. Her clothes spread wide,
> And mermaid-like a while they bore her up:
> Which time she chanted snatches of old tunes,
> As one incapable of her own distress,
> Or like a creature native and indued
> Unto that element: but long it could not be
> Till that her garments, heavy with their drink,
> Pull'd the poor wretch from her melodious lay
> To muddy death.

Laertes is unable to control his grief. When he leaves, Claudius tells Gertrude that he must once more attempt to calm Laertes' rage.

ACT V

In a churchyard, two gravediggers are at work. They are talking about the questionable death of Ophelia and wondering whether it will be considered a suicide, in which case she would not be granted a Christian burial, or an accident.

While the second gravedigger goes to fetch a pot of liquor, Hamlet and Horatio enter and hear the first gravedigger singing a ballad as he digs. Hamlet asks Horatio:

> Has this fellow no feeling of his business, that he sings at grave-making?
>
> **Horatio:** Custom hath made it in him a property of easiness.

The gravedigger casually throws up a skull, and Hamlet begins to reflect upon death as the great leveller of all people:

> That skull had a tongue in it, and could sing once: how the knave jowls it to the ground, as if it were Cain's jaw-bone, that did the first murder! It might be the pate of a politician, which this ass now o'erreaches; one that would circumvent God, might it not?

Hamlet then questions the gravedigger, who answers in chop-logic, a kind of reasoning in which the speaker confines himself only to a special meaning of a given word or phrase.

Upon further questioning, the gravedigger identifies one skull as that of Yorick, King Hamlet's jester and a favorite of young Hamlet. Hamlet picks up the skull and sadly remarks:

> Alas, poor Yorick! I knew him, Horatio: a fellow of infinite jest, of most excellent fancy: he hath borne me on his back a thousand times; and now how abhorred in my imagination it is! my gorge rises at it. Here hung those lips that I have kissed I know not how oft. Where be your gibes now? your gambols? your songs? your flashes of merriment, that were wont to set the table on a roar? Not one now, to mock your own grinning? quite chop-fallen? Now get you to my lady's chamber, and tell her, let her

paint an inch thick, to this favour she must come; make her laugh at that.

A funeral procession, the members of which include the king, the queen and Laertes, enters. Hamlet and Horatio step back, unobserved. Laertes complains about the limited rites given to his dead sister, and a priest responds that this is more than she deserves, considering the doubtful circumstances of her death.

As Ophelia is lowered into the grave, the queen scatters flowers over her body and says:

Sweets to the sweet: farewell!
I hoped thou shouldst have been my Hamlet's wife;
I thought thy bride-bed to have deck'd, sweet maid,
And not have strew'd thy grave.

Laertes cries out in grief and leaps into the grave, asking that he be buried with his sister. Hamlet steps forward and demands to know:

What is he whose grief
Bears such an emphasis? whose phrase of sorrow
Conjures the wandering stars and makes them stand
Like wonder-wounded hearers?

Hamlet also leaps into the grave, and a struggle between him and Laertes follows. Attendants part them, and the queen asks Hamlet the reason for his conduct. He replies:

I loved Ophelia: forty thousand brothers
Could not, with all their quantity of love,
Make up my sum. What wilt thou do for her?

Hamlet now asks Laertes, "What is the reason that you use me thus? / I loved you ever." The king manages to convince Laertes to remain patient and wait to receive his revenge during the fencing match.

Hamlet now has the time and opportunity to tell Horatio about his experiences on the ship. During his first night at sea, he learned that Claudius had planned to have him killed.

Hamlet changed Claudius' written instructions so that Rosencrantz and Guildenstern would be put to death upon their arrival in England. The next day, the pirates attacked the ship, as Hamlet informed Horatio in his letter, but only Hamlet was taken captive. The others proceeded on their voyage to England. Horatio is shocked to learn of the extent of Claudius' villainy. He then points out that Claudius will soon discover what has happened to Rosencrantz and Guildenstern, but Hamlet replies that he is safe for the present.

Osric, a messenger from the king, brings Hamlet news of the wager the king has placed upon his ability in the fencing match. Hamlet is to proceed at once to the place arranged for the match.

When they are alone again, Horatio doubts that Hamlet will win the wager. He advises the prince to excuse himself from the match by saying he is unprepared. Hamlet responds:

> Not a whit; we defy augury: there is special providence in the fall of a sparrow. If it be now, 'tis not to come; if it be not to come, it will be now; if it be not now, yet it will come: the readiness is all; since no man has aught of what he leaves, what is 't to leave betimes? Let be.

The entrance of the king, the queen, Laertes, Osric and other court members is the signal for the beginning of the fencing bout. As Laertes and Hamlet shake hands, Hamlet begs Laertes' pardon for anything he has done. His rash action must be blamed on his madness, something done when he was not himself. Laertes states, in turn, that it is only his honor which holds him now to the bout. Revenge is no longer his motive. Finally, Laertes says:

> I do receive your offer'd love like love
> And will not wrong it.
> **Hamlet:** I embrace it freely,
> And will this brother's wager frankly play.
> Give us the foils. Come on.

The contestants choose their swords, and, before the match begins, the king announces:

Set me the stoups of wine upon that table.
If Hamlet give the first or second hit,
Or quit in answer of the third exchange,
Let all the battlements their ordnance fire;
The king shall drink to Hamlet's better breath;
And in the cup an union shall he throw,
Richer than that which four successive kings
In Denmark's crown have worn. Give me the cups;
And let the kettle to the trumpet speak,
The trumpet to the cannoneer without,
The cannons to the heavens, the heaven to earth,
'Now the king drinks to Hamlet.'

Hamlet scores the first hit, and Claudius drinks to his health. He also offers Hamlet a drink, which the prince refuses for the time being. During the match, Gertrude, much to Claudius' distress, picks up the poisoned cup and drinks to Hamlet's fortune. She then wipes Hamlet's face and offers him a drink, but he refuses again.

When the match resumes, Laertes wounds Hamlet with the poisoned sword. A struggle follows, the weapons are exchanged and Hamlet wounds Laertes with the poisoned weapon. Realizing that he is about to die, Laertes acknowledges that he is "justly killed with [his] own treachery." Gertrude falls, but she lives long enough to exclaim, "The drink, the drink! I am poison'd." Hamlet orders that the doors be locked and that the treachery be revealed. Laertes explains before he dies:

Hamlet, thou art slain;
No medicine in the world can do thee good,
In thee there is not half an hour of life;
The treacherous instrument is in thy hand,
Unbated and envenom'd: the foul practice
Hath turn'd itself on me; lo, here I lie,
Never to rise again: thy mother's poison'd:
I can no more: the king, the king's to blame.

Enraged, Hamlet finally stabs the king and forces him to swallow the rest of the poisoned drink. Turning to Horatio, Hamlet makes a last request: "report me and my cause aright / To the unsatisfied." Hearing the approach of Fortinbras' army, Hamlet speaks his final words:

I cannot live to hear the news from England;
But I do prophesy the election lights
On Fortinbras: he has my dying voice;
So tell him, with the occurrents, more and less,
Which have solicited. The rest is silence.

Horatio pays tribute to the dead prince:

Now cracks a noble heart. Good night, sweet prince,
And flights of angels sing thee to thy rest!

The sound of a march is heard, and Fortinbras, returned from his expedition against the Poles, enters. At the same time, the English ambassadors come with news of the execution of Rosencrantz and Guildenstern. Horatio offers to explain "how these things came about":

. . . so shall you hear
Of carnal, bloody and unnatural acts,
Of accidental judgements, casual slaughters,
Of deaths put on by cunning and forced cause,
And, in this upshot, purposes mistook
Fall'n on the inventors' heads: all this can I
Truly deliver.

Fortinbras, in the closing lines of the play, orders an honorable burial for Hamlet:

Let four captains
Bear Hamlet, like a soldier, to the stage;
For he was likely, had he been put on,
To have proved most royally: and, for his passage,
The soldiers' music and the rites of war
Speak loudly for him.
Take up the bodies: such a sight as this
Becomes the field, but here shows much amiss.
Go, bid the soldiers shoot.

Part B: Questions and Answers by Act and Scene

ACT I • SCENE 1

Question 1.

How are the first entrance of the ghost (line 40) and its second exit (lines 137-157) made impressive?

Answer

The ghost makes its appearance as Bernardo is about to tell his already tense listeners of its previous visits. It departs when a rooster crows, according to superstition that spirits do not move about in daylight. It is reluctant to speak to Horatio and the other lesser characters.

Question 2.

Modern productions of *Hamlet* usually have the ghost visible to the audience. What is gained — or lost — by having it actually on stage?

Answer

To have it appear on stage heightens the dramatic effect and makes the atmosphere more tense.

Question 3.

Why did the officers of the guard invite Horatio to join them in the night's watch?

Answer

Horatio has been a fellow student of Prince Hamlet and is now his most intimate friend. A scholar, he can speak to the ghost in Latin, the only language in which, it was then supposed, communication could be held with spirits. Above all, he is a man of high character and acknowledged judgment, whose opinions will be listened to by all and whose evidence will be regarded as almost conclusive.

Question 4.

Mention any superstitions connected with ghosts referred to in this scene.

Answer

Superstitions referred to in this scene are the notions that: (1) Latin has power over ghosts; (2) the appearance of ghosts warns of coming disaster; (3) any person crossing the spot on which a spirit has been seen becomes subject to its influence; (4) spirits and ghosts glide by night about the place where, in their life on earth, they had hoarded treasure; (5) spirits do not move about after daybreak; (6) at Christmas, no spirits dare to stir abroad.

Question 5.

Give the context and explain the meaning of the following passage:

A little ere the mightiest Julius fell.

Answer

In the opening scene of the play, after the first appearance of the ghost to Horatio, Marcellus and Bernardo, a discussion takes place between the three watchers concerning the troubled state of Denmark. Bernardo thinks it is significant that the spirit of the late king should come armed through their watch. He sees a kind of fitness in the appearance of the "portentous figure" at a time of nightly toil and warlike preparation. Horatio, the scholar returned from Wittenberg, is troubled by the spirit, and he imagines it to be prophesying "fierce events." He describes the strange and wonderful sights seen. "A little ere the mightiest Julius fell." The dead arose, and ominous signs such as "stars with trains of fire and dews of blood," appeared in the sky, and the moon "was sick almost to doomsday with eclipse."

The reference, therefore, is to omens that occurred in Rome before the murder of Julius Caesar by Brutus and his fellow conspirators.

ACT I • SCENE 2

Question 1.

How does Claudius attempt to justify his hasty marriage

to the queen?

Answer

The king tries to justify his conduct on the grounds of convenience. It is, for him, a mark of wisdom to act contrary to nature if such action enhances his own comfort and power. He is not ashamed even to boast of his conduct, which he calls discretion and which consists of a wise moderating grief with considerations of self-gratification, "in equal scale weighing delight and dole."

Question 2.

After the somber background of the opening scene, the first part of Scene 2 forms a colorful and striking contrast. Discuss this statement.

Answer

The courtiers provide colorful costumes in this scene, which is the first state occasion for the new king. The period of mourning is over, and the court is gay. We are brought from an eerie world of darkness and ghosts into one of cheerful reality.

Question 3.

What impression does Claudius make in his first speech?

Answer

Claudius is clever, suave, shrewd, plausible and excessive. He also seems to dote on Gertrude. He evidently has been able to deceive the court, but Shakespeare presents him so that the audience is prepared to dislike him.

Question 4.

What indications are in Claudius' speech of the "rottenness" in the state of Denmark?

Answer

We have already heard the king's miserable self-justification of his marriage to the queen. We now have the further evidence of rottenness, in the statement that young Fortinbras considered the state "to be disjoint and out of frame" and, therefore, ripe for invasion.

Question 5.

Is Hamlet brooding over the death of his father, as the king and queen think?

Answer

There is no question that Claudius thinks Hamlet, who sits aside, brooding and clothed all in black, is still in mourning for his father. The king tries to cheer the melancholy prince from his sorrow, not only by pointing out that nature's "common theme is death of fathers," but also by assuring Hamlet that he looks upon the prince as his own son and heir, "the most immediate to our throne."

When we listen to Hamlet's own words, however, as he voices his innermost thoughts in his soliloquy, the true source of his trouble becomes evident. His entire outburst rages about his mother's marriage. She has remarried with "most wicked speed." She has joined herself to a man not worthy of comparison with her first husband. She has, furthermore, married within the bounds of an incestuous relationship. Whatever may be burdening Hamlet's mind — his natural melancholy, the sense that he has been deprived of his proper place as king, or even a suspicion that his father's sudden death was not an accident — it is the picture of a beloved and happily married mother rushing into another man's arms as soon as her husband dies that has most deeply wounded the prince and overturned the values of his world.

Question 6.

What is Laertes' reason for wishing to return to France?

Answer

We may suppose France to have been, in Hamlet's time, as it is now, famous for its culture and elegance. We have Polonius' statement (Act I, Scene 3) that France set the fashion in matters of dress, while Claudius (Act IV, Scene 7) speaks of the nation as possessing wonderful powers of horsemanship. Laertes' boasted skill in fencing is the result of much practice against the best French masters. It is only natural, then, that the active and showy Laertes should be eager to return to a country, the customs of which are so likely to satisfy his own pleasure. Later, the student, Hamlet, shows a comparable, yet more serious, inclination to return to Wittenberg, the home of philosophic study.

Question 7.

How does Hamlet receive from Horatio the news of the appearance of his father's ghost?

Answer

For once, Hamlet's conversation is simple and direct. He is carried out of the region of meditation and philosophy. His language is abrupt, and his questions are practical and to the point. He demands particulars and details, and, as long as his friends are present, "his soul sits still." There is neither argument nor sceptical distrust in Hamlet's reaction, but only the resolve to speak to the ghost and the determination to maintain secrecy in the meantime.

Question 8.

What is the state of Hamlet's mind before his interview with the ghost? Is there any reason for supposing that he, at that time, had any suspicion of the true cause of his father's death?

Answer

Hamlet is overwhelmed with grief for the loss of his beloved father. We have seen him unwillingly plunged into the pomp and pageantry of a corrupt court while his thoughts remain fixed upon the perfections of his noble father, whom, "with vailed lids," he appears to be forever remembering. He has been overruled in his desire to return to the academic seclusion of Wittenberg. He has been cheated out of his rightful inheritance and he is naturally indignant at being compelled to live in the hated surroundings of the court. He has suddenly become convinced that his mother, whom he had loved, is unworthy of his affection. All this has made him weary of life. All earthly things appear "stale, flat, and unprofitable," and he longs for death. But, after his interview with Horatio, we see other feelings force themselves upon his naturally unsuspicious mind. He has already felt doubts and forewarnings of disaster: now, for the first time, he speaks of them. "All is not well," he says, suspecting foul play. His mind is full of suppressed emotions and it is prepared to see visions or communicate with the spiritual and the unknown.

Question 9.

Describe two significant qualities of Hamlet revealed in the scene in which he appears for the first time in the play, and show how these qualities are made clear to the audience.

Answer

Hamlet does not make his first appearance in this play until line 65 of Act I, Scene 2. His opening remark, "A little more than kin, and less than kind," is in the form of an aside, a melancholy and bitter reflection on his relationship with Claudius. His love of puns is shown in the rapidity with which he catches on to Claudius' reference to "clouds" and rejects the sense while sustaining the figure of speech in the word "sun" — here symbolizing the royal court of Claudius. His intention is clear, though indirectly expressed: "I am having to see a great deal too much of you!" This dislike of Claudius is a significant quality of Hamlet.

An equally significant quality of Hamlet is his deep love and grief for his father, which he maintains to an extreme degree. He is criticized for this, by both his mother and her second husband. He promises not to return immediately to the University of Wittenberg, an act that shows a measure of filial respect.

Hamlet's philosophic nature is also demonstrated in the language, imagery and feeling of the soliloquy, beginning "O, that this too too sullied flesh would melt." Here, his hatred for and suspicion of Claudius become obvious.

ACT I • SCENE 3

Question 1.

What view does Laertes take of Hamlet's relationship with Ophelia?

Answer

Laertes is probably incapable of understanding a mind as

pure as Hamlet's, and would consider that trifling with a young girl's affections is but "a taint of liberty," not dishonor. Evidently, he thinks Hamlet is merely flirting with Ophelia for the sake of his own amusement. Perhaps he loves her now, Laertes says, but it is clear that he does not think Hamlet will maintain anything more than a temporary attachment, "sweet not lasting, the perfume and suppliance of a minute."

Question 2.

What impressions do you get of the characters of Laertes and Ophelia from Scene 3?

Answer

Laertes is wordy, self-righteous, a bit wild, conceited and young. Ophelia is innocent, lovable, weak and obedient to her father and brother.

Question 3.

Is Laertes' warning to Ophelia justified in view of subsequent events?

Answer

Our knowledge of Hamlet's character convinces us that Laertes entirely misjudges the nature of the prince's sentiments toward Ophelia. But it was not in this respect alone that Laertes' judgment is at fault. He looks upon marriage between Hamlet and Ophelia as a political impossibility. Later events prove that the queen would have welcomed such a connection, while Hamlet's personal popularity with the people of Denmark would have ensured their approval of any alliance he might have chosen to make.

ACT I • SCENE 4

Question 1.

Show that Hamlet is superior in refinement to the age in which he lives.

Answer

In this scene, Hamlet expresses contempt for the

wildness of the generation and the drunkenness that robs the Danish nation of the praise that its achievements might otherwise win. Morally upright himself, he hates the hypocrisy of his uncle; truthful himself, he scorns the cunning and scheming of Polonius and the pretentious ways of Osric. He also despises and ridicules the treachery of Rosencrantz and Guildenstern. He singles out as his friend the student, Horatio, who is more like an ancient Roman than a Dane. Hamlet speaks about literature, takes pleasure in the company of artists and recites poetry. All his uncertainty proceeds from the conflict of his inherent gentleness and fine moral feelings with the stern duty of revenge imposed upon him by his father's ghost.

Question 2.

Show that Hamlet, when excited, is capable of independent action.

Answer

In spite of all that Horatio and Marcellus do to prevent Hamlet from following the ghost, he nevertheless persists in his resolve to hear it and follows after it. Being "desperate with imagination," he fears neither death nor danger to his soul.

Question 3.

Comment on the style and versification of Scene 4.

Answer

Lines 17-38 are involved, philosophical and difficult for an audience to follow. Moreover, they do not help to forward the plot. For these reasons, probably, they were omitted from the First Folio. In the rest of the scene, one cannot fail to be struck by the rapid, dramatic nature of the speeches. Short, jerky, simple sentences quickly follow one another, and are suggestive of coldness, excitement and fear of the supernatural. These traits are less marked in Horatio, perhaps, than in any of the other watchers in the night.

ACT I • SCENE 5

Question 1.

What seems to be Shakespeare's conception of ghosts in Scene 5? Compare the ghost in *Hamlet* with other ghosts in Shakespeare's plays.

Answer

Shakespeare uses ghosts to further plot, create atmosphere and to reveal character. Ghosts in *Macbeth* and *Julius Caesar* are usually seen only by someone with an affinity for them, as in *Hamlet*. The ghost in *Hamlet* is not just a creation of a disturbed mind, as is the case in *Richard III* and in the appearance of Banquo's ghost in *Macbeth*.

Question 2.

Show that Hamlet is willing to accomplish the required deed of vengeance.

Answer

Upon the departure of the ghost, Hamlet swears that he will wipe from his memory all the thoughts of his youth, and that the ghost's "commandment all alone shall live within the book and volume of his brain." The ghost finds him "apt." Indeed, in the excitement of the moment, he feels so himself. He does not fear death. The voice of his sensitive conscience is still, and he longs for the moment when, "with wings as swift as meditation, or the thoughts of love," he may sweep to his revenge.

Question 3.

How soon after the interview with the ghost does Hamlet decide to feign madness?

Answer

A great change in the character of Hamlet is the immediate result of his supernatural visitation. He knows that he has experienced a shock to his nature that almost unhinged his mind. This awareness of insanity suggests to his active mind the device of feigning madness. On being rejoined by Horatio and Marcellus, he swears them to secrecy and begs them not "to note that they know aught of him," as he "perchance hereafter shall think meet to put an antic disposition on."

Question 4.

What do you suppose to have been Hamlet's purpose in feigning madness?

Answer

His purpose seems to have been to gain more freedom of action and to escape the too-close observation of those whom he himself wished to watch. We shall see later, however, that he defeated his own purpose and that his eccentricities caused the king to regard him with fear and suspicion, and to spy on his actions.

Question 5.

How far has the action of the plot been carried in Act I?

Answer

Hamlet is aware of Claudius' treachery and has promised to avenge the murder of his father. But, according to the last speech of the act, he is not sure he is fit to carry out the task.

ACT II • SCENE 1

Question 1.

How is Polonius' crafty, suspicious and insincere nature shown in this scene?

Answer

The dishonorable errand upon which he sends Reynaldo to Paris is evidence of his suspicious nature. His indirect methods and cunning contrivances for obtaining knowledge of his son's actions could only have proceeded from the mind of a crafty politician. His insincerity is shown in the fact that his real anxiety is not for the purity of his son's character, but merely for the correctness of his outward behavior.

Question 2.

Explain the strange conduct of Hamlet during his

meeting with Ophelia.

Answer

Hamlet has sworn to wipe away from his mind all thoughts that might interfere with his revenge. Therefore, the sentiment of love must have no place in his mind. He seeks out Ophelia so that he may give her up in order to assume his new character. The interview is a silent one. The silence is a token of the depths of his love for her. He does not speak, in case he should betray his real feelings, but he gazes at her long and lovingly, as if to impress on his imagination the image of her face. A sigh, "so piteous and profound as it did seem to shatter all his bulk and end his being," shows us what giving up Ophelia cost him.

Question 3.

Answer *briefly* the questions below about the following passage:

But breathe his faults so quaintly
That they may seem the taints of liberty
(Act II, Scene 1, 31)

(i) By whom is this said, to whom and about whom?
(ii) On what occasion is it said?
(iii) What answer is given later to the question?
Where should this action be carried out?
(iv) Explain "taints of liberty."

Answer

(i) By Polonius to Reynaldo about Laertes.

(ii) On the occasion of Reynaldo's departure for Paris, where he will meet with Laertes, to whom he is to give some money and some notes.

(iii) The purpose Polonius had in view was to worm out, by indirect means, the secrets of Laertes' life in Paris, a scheme thus expressed by Polonius: "Your bait of falsehood takes this carp of truth."

(iv) This expression refers to the indiscretions that are natural to one who is enjoying full liberty for the first time in his life.

ACT II • SCENE 2

Question 1.

What part in the plot is played by Rosencrantz and Guildenstern? Do they successfully carry out the king's designs? If not, what is the reason of their failure?

Answer

The use to which the king intends to put these two courtiers is set forth in his opening speech. That they unskilfully act their part and are unsuccessful in learning from Hamlet the reason for his odd behavior will be seen in their first interview with him. Hamlet himself supplies the reason for their failure when he declares that there is "a kind of confession in their looks which their modesties have not craft enough to colour." He sees, at once, that they have been sent to spy upon him.

Question 2.

How does Polonius pay tribute to the intellectual power of Hamlet under the disguise of madness?

Answer

Polonius is struck by Hamlet's keen wit and says, in an aside, "How pregnant sometimes his replies are! a happiness that often madness hits on, which reason and sanity could not so prosperously be delivered of." Polonius has already been obliged to confess that "though this be madness, yet there's method in it."

Question 3.

What dramatic purpose is served by the introduction of the players?

Answer

The travelling players, who visit Elsinore and talk at length to Hamlet, give Shakespeare a chance to voice his opinion on acting and the theater.

The players' arrival inspires Hamlet to stage a play that bears a close resemblance to his father's murder. He wants to be sure of Claudius' guilt and he says that "The play's the thing. Wherein I'll catch the conscience of the king." The evidence obtained causes Hamlet to act impulsively by killing "the good old man" behind the arras, whom he "mistook for his betters."

Thus, the visit of the players reveals Shakespeare's interests, establishes Claudius' guilt and leads directly to the events of the tragedy.

Question 4.

How did the practice of introducing children on the stage originate?

Answer

This practice first originated with the "children of St. Paul's," of whom the earliest mention is made in 1569. These children of St. Paul's, acting behind the Convocation House, presented plays in which the Puritans were laughed at. Such plays were suppressed because of the personal abuse introduced into their comedies. But, about 1600, the removal of the ban resulted in the revival of the plays at St. Paul's. The poets used performances of children as a vehicle of abuse. From deriding the Puritans, they came to ridicule the stage itself, thus exclaiming "against their own succession." When *Hamlet* was written, they abused even Shakespeare's theater, the Globe. This is why they are criticized in *Hamlet.*

Question 5.

Describe briefly the scene that is depicted by the player.

Answer

For a full description, see Virgil's *AEneid* (Book II Part 2 310-566). Pyrrhus, Achilles' son, has entered, with his Danaan comrades, Priam's city of Ilium. The city is devastated. Pyrrhus bursts into the presence of the old king, who, trembling with age, had hopelessly dressed himself in his long-disused armor and raised his sword. Pyrrhus shrinks, for one moment, from the outrageous deed. Then, without pity, he thrusts his sword to the hilt into Priam's side. Hecuba, overcome with grief, appeals to the heavens with such pitiful cries that the gods themselves must have been moved to tears.

Question 6.

What new ideas suggest themselves here to Hamlet's doubting mind?

Answer

Since Hamlet received from the ghost his first impulse to action, he has allowed so much time to elapse without performing anything that he now begins to think it possible he may have been deceived by the "honest ghost," and that the spirit may have been nothing more than the devil, disguised as his father. He decides to have "grounds more relative than this" and to "catch the conscience of the king" by means of a play that shall represent something like the murder of his father.

Question 7.

Explain the following passage and its context:

What's Hecuba to him.

Answer

These words occur in the soliloquy spoken by Hamlet just after he has dismissed the strolling players. The first player has recited a speech from an old play, in which the death of Priam at the hands of Pyrrhus and the consequent grief and "burst of clamour" by Hecuba, Priam's wife, are set forth in moving language. Hamlet has seen the player affected by the recital of the poetic fiction to such a degree

That from her working all his visage wann'd;
Tears in his eyes, distraction in's aspect,
A broken voice, and his whole function suiting
With forms to his conceit ? and all for nothing!
For Hecuba!

"What's Hecuba to him, or he to Hecuba?" wonders Hamlet. He then asks, "what would the player do had he the motive and the cue for passion that he himself had." He heaps scorn upon his own head, calls himself "a dull and muddy-mettled rascal," a John-a-dreams, pigeon-livered and a coward, lacking "gall to make oppression bitter." This self-abuse shows the violence of thought and language to which he can be moved by the speech of a mere player "in a fiction, in a dream of passion."

Question 8.

Why is so much of this act written in prose?

Answer

Whenever prose is used by Shakespeare, it is always for some purpose of contrast. Most commonly, it is used as the recognized medium for the low characters, in order to provide comic relief. In this act, most of the prose is of a higher character than that. In the early part of the act, it shows the contrast between Hamlet, when he is his natural self, and Hamlet, when he has assumed madness. In conversation with Rosencrantz and Guildenstern, there is the contrast between Hamlet, the fellow student, and Hamlet, the prince. In conversation with the players, there are two reasons for the use of prose: (1) to mark the degree of familiarity that existed between Hamlet and his old friend; (2) to strengthen the contrast between the dramatic play of *Hamlet* and the epic tragedy of Gonzago.

Some of the prose in this act, (297-311, "I have of late," etc.) is very elaborate and is more full of concentrated meaning than almost any of the blank verse of this play.

Question 9.

Comment on the language used in the player's speech.

Answer

It has been objected that the player's speech is pompous, undramatic and merely ridiculous. It also has been suggested that it was introduced merely as burlesque. This is not so. In order to distinguish, by its style, the play-within-the-play from the real play, Shakespeare has chosen epic narrative, which is not intended to be dramatic. He has gone back to an epic period, the period of Æneas and Dido, which did not lend itself to dramatic treatment. Although high-sounding rhetoric is intermingled with the poetry and some of the metaphors are almost absurd, many of the lines are impressive. Whatever we may think of the language, it is certain that Shakespeare himself did not intend, in his player's play, to ridicule the style of any contemporary dramatist.

ACT III • SCENE I

Question 1.

What is the theme upon which Hamlet meditates in the famous soliloquy, beginning "To be, or not to be"?

Answer

Hamlet is here meditating upon the undeserved sufferings endured by mankind, upon the mysteries of death and upon the tendency of thought to weaken the power of action.

Question 2.

Account for Hamlet's apparently rude and harsh behavior to Ophelia.

Answer

Hamlet's bitter words are directed, not against Ophelia, but against women in general. He tells the innocent girl of the faults and weaknesses of her sex. To Ophelia, the harshest thing he says is, "Be thou as chaste as ice, as pure as snow, thou shalt not escape calumny." He is genuinely disturbed by the unexpected presence of one he loves. To this is added, as Charles Lamb expresses it, "a profound artifice of love to alienate Ophelia by affected discourtesies, so to prepare her mind for the breaking off of that loving intercourse which can no longer find a place amidst business so serious as that which he has to do."

Question 3.

Show that Hamlet is innocent of all the vices of which he accuses himself before Ophelia.

Answer

That Hamlet is not proud is shown by the favor in which he is held by the common people, by his friendship with the poor scholar, Horatio, by his love for the sweet, yet simple, Ophelia and by his absence of all ambition. That vengefulness forms no part of his character is made evident throughout the play by the fact that he cannot commit an act of vengeance, even when that act has become a matter of duty and religion to him. That he is not ambitious is shown by the readiness with which he allows his claim to the throne of Denmark to be set aside, by his own statement that he "could be bounded in a nut-shell and count himself a king of infinite space" and by his constant feeling of his own nothingness.

Question 4.

How does the king's reaction to what he overhears as a "lawful espial" contrast with Hamlet's customary behavior?

Answer

The king immediately decides that Hamlet is to be sent to England. He is prompt, vigorous and decisive in dealing at once with possible danger.

Question 5.

Point to some of the principal metaphors in Hamlet's speech (Act III, Scene 1, 53-85) and show how they record various stages of one train of thought.

Answer

Life is represented by the familiar image of a contest. Hamlet makes metaphorical mention of various operations of war: slings and arrows, take up arms, shocks, hindrances, oppressors, suffering, self-destruction, sweating under burdens, flight, endurance, cowardice and great enterprise.

ACT III • SCENE 2

Question 1.

What are the faults against which Hamlet warns the players?

Answer

Briefly, the faults of actors here condemned are those of loudness, ranting, woodenness, grotesque contortions, mispronunciation of words and speaking more than is set down in the play.

Question 2.

Show that Hamlet admired in Horatio those qualities that he himself lacked.

Answer

The qualities in Horatio that Hamlet praises are his common sense, his justice, consistency, coolness and frankness. With these qualities may be contrasted Hamlet's overactive imagination, his impulsiveness, indecision, excitability and complex nature. Horatio is matter-of-fact and prosaic; Hamlet is overflowing with poetry and philosophy.

Question 3.

"Where joy most revels, grief doth most lament." Show how Hamlet's character illustrates this statement.

Answer

Many instances may be given of Hamlet's rapid transition from melancholy and despair to merriment and humor. Deeply agitated by his interviews with the ghost, he returns to his friends only to surprise them by his jests and witty remarks. (Act I, Scene 5). Another time, when, oppressed with melancholy (Act II, Scene 2, 169), he meets Polonius, his mood changes and he fools the older man brilliantly. As a spectator of the tragic play that means so much to him and to the king, his wit and humor are evident in trivial conversation with Ophelia (Act III, Scene 2). After the play, he recites a pleasant verse to Horatio. He can joke in the presence of death in the graveyard and, at the sight of Laertes' grief, he is overcome at once by tragic passion. (Act V, Scene 1).

Question 4.

What is in Hamlet's mind when he prays that the soul of Nero may never enter his bosom?

Answer

Hamlet remembers that Nero murdered his mother, Agrippina. Hamlet's mind is worked up to a frenzy of almost uncontrollable passion and he fears that the Devil may gain power over him. His naturally mild and gentle nature shrinks from violent impulses, and he prays to be delivered from the possibility of matricide.

Question 5.

Explain the following passage:

The lady doth protest too much.

Answer

The play is in progress upon the miniature stage. The player-king, sensing the approach of his own death, expresses a hope that his queen might find a second husband whose love for her may prove no less than his own. The queen resents the idea of ever taking a second husband. When the king suggests that time may change her opinions, she breaks out into passionate protest against what, to her now, appears the unforgivable crime of second marriage. She prays that she may suffer darkness, misery, despair and lasting strife if, once a widow, she ever marries again. The player-king then sleeps, and Hamlet asks his mother, "Madam, how like you this play?" to which she replies, "The lady doth protest too much, methinks." King Claudius shows signs of alarm, but the queen gives no indication that she is aware of any comment upon her. We may, therefore, conclude that she is innocent of any participation in, or knowledge of, the murder of her husband.

ACT III • SCENE 3

Question 1.

Show that the king has a conscience.

Answer

No man can completely subdue the voice of conscience within him. More than once, we have seen that the king's crime brought with it a hard burden to bear. "How smart a lash" Polonius innocently gave to the conscience of the king in Act III, Scene 1, 49-50. What agony he suffered as he sat a silent spectator of *The Murder of Gonzago*. What anguish was in that "bosom black as death" when his guilty soul struggled vainly to free itself by confession through prayer.

Question 2.

State and comment upon Hamlet's reason for not murdering the king when at prayer.

Answer

This refusal to kill the king is a part of Hamlet's weakness. His excuse that revenge performed while the criminal was at prayer would be "hire and salary, not revenge" and that to postpone the deed would only prolong his sickly days are merely excuses for not acting when the opportunity presents itself. The real reasons for the hesitation lie in Hamlet's indecision and "poor validity of purpose." It may also be that what Hamlet wants is, not private revenge, but public justice.

ACT III • SCENE 4

Question 1.

"Thou find'st to be too busy in some danger." How is this a striking summary of Polonius' character?

Answer

He has interfered in Ophelia's, Laertes' and Hamlet's lives. He has delighted in eavesdropping and in meddling. Now he is paid off for these acts.

Question 2.

Is it good drama to have the ghost appear again at this time? What do you think of Shakespeare's practice of having the ghost visible to some characters but not to others? Is the same practice followed in any other Shakespearean play?

Answer

The ghost's second appearance gives a certain unity to the plot and reminds us of the duty placed on Hamlet. It shows an affinity between Hamlet and the ghost that is lacking between it and Gertrude. This same practice is followed in *Macbeth*, where only Macbeth sees Banquo's ghost, and in *Julius Caesar*, where the guards do not see Caesar's ghost.

Question 3.

Describe the effect upon the queen of Hamlet's harsh words.

Answer

She is first angry, then alarmed and then, in turn, remorseful, compassionate, subdued, obedient and almost loving.

Question 4.

What evidence is there that the queen had no previous knowledge of King Hamlet's murder by Claudius? What is the extent of her guilt?

Answer

The problem of his mother's guilt deeply troubled Hamlet. Even before his encounter with the ghost, he felt that she was at fault. Therefore, in his mother's chamber, Hamlet responds to his stabbing of Polonius and the queen's shocked cry, "Oh, what a rash and bloody deed is this!" with a stern accusation:

> A bloody deed! Almost as bad, good mother,
> As kill a king and marry with his brother.

This is the crucial moment. In this one outcry, Hamlet unloads his overburdened soul.

What, then, is Gertrude's answer? Knowing that words of protest will sound empty, will have no force of proof, Shakespeare leaves it to the actress to portray the surprised reaction of the queen. Gertrude's words in response to Hamlet's are an echo: "As kill a king!" The actress must behave either like a woman caught and confused in her guilt or like an innocent woman overwhelmed by the accusation. Most actresses, of course, seek audience sympathy by adopting the latter tone. Gertrude may have succumbed to Claudius' loving advances, but she was no partner in, and did not even suspect, her husband's murder.

That Shakespeare wished Hamlet to draw the conclusion that his mother was not involved in the murder may be judged from the fact that, throughout the rest of their talk,

Hamlet's words deal only with the great contrast between the two men she has married, and Gertrude is deeply affected by the memory Hamlet wakens of her first husband.

At no time does Gertrude admit — or even attempt to deny — guilt either of adultery or murder. She is upset, however, at Hamlet's picture of her passion and lust, and of the villainy and lechery of Claudius. She seems full of remorse for her hasty and incestuous marriage. She also promises — and keeps her promise — not to reveal Hamlet's thoughts to Claudius.

Question 5.

How does Hamlet attempt to console himself for the murder of Polonius?

Answer

Hamlet, looking down at his victim, excuses himself thus: "I must be cruel, only to be kind." He regards himself as heaven's instrument of justice. He has been compelled to do the murder, and this compulsion has been a punishment for him, as well as for his victim.

Question 6.

How is the queen's evident affection for Hamlet shown in this act?

Answer

Her pity for Hamlet is genuine, and so is her desire to conceal from the king all information that might turn him against her son. She addresses Hamlet in affectionate terms, and Polonius refers to her evident affection for her son. Hamlet, in spite of his anger, reflects in his language to her the love she feels for him. In a later scene, we shall hear the king, speaking of Hamlet, confess that "the queen, his mother, lives almost by his looks."

Question 7.

Why does Hamlet choose to sit by Ophelia, rather than by his mother?

Answer

When Queen Gertrude invites her son to sit by her, he responds, "Here's metal more attractive" and goes over to lie beside Ophelia, putting his head upon her lap. Probably a mixture of emotions caused him to choose to sit by the girl.

In the first place, Hamlet seems to have loved Ophelia and to have suffered at having to part from her — whether that parting was caused solely by her father's command or by his own sense that he could not impose upon her gentle nature his grim burden of revenge. His feelings toward her are further complicated by his knowledge that, in her weakness of will, she has been used as a decoy to sound out his thoughts and intentions. Under such complex circumstances, it is natural that he should be glad of an opportunity to be near Ophelia, while, at the same time, be bitter enough to make coarse jokes at her expense.

We must further consider that Hamlet is still deeply disturbed by his mother's hasty and, in his mind, unwise marriage. To accept her invitation to sit beside her would seem acceptance also of her present situation, so that he would have to stifle still more his resentment, which he can, to some extent, relieve in his twisted remarks to Ophelia. For example, "Look you how cheerfully my mother looks, and my father died within these two hours" is an expression of bitterness on Hamlet's part.

Finally, Hamlet's purpose at the play is to watch the king's reaction. Since the queen is undoubtedly seated beside her spouse, Hamlet will have a more direct view of the king's face if he sits apart from them.

ACT IV • SCENE I

Question 1.

How does the king receive the news of Polonius' death? What aspects of his character do his remarks illustrate?

Answer

Consideration for his own safety is his first thought: "It had been so with us, had we been there." He expresses no sorrow for his lost counsellor. Instead, his imagination busies itself at once with the practical question, "how shall this bloody deed be answered?" The quickness of his understanding in cases where his own safety is concerned is further displayed by the readiness with which he forms his plans for the future and devises a scheme to draw suspicion away from himself.

Question 2.

What course does the king decide to adopt upon hearing of Polonius' death?

Answer

He decides upon two courses: (1) to hasten the preparation for Hamlet's banishment to England; (2) to secure the agreement and participation of his counsellors in his plans, in order to remove suspicion from himself.

Question 3.

Write short answers to the questions below about the following passage:

> this vile deed
> We must, with all our majesty and skill,
> Both countenance and excuse

(i) What "vile deed" is referred to?
(ii) Why should it be countenanced and excused?
(iii) How and to whom is it subsequently excused?

Answer

(i) The reference is to the slaying of Polonius by Hamlet.

(ii) Claudius gives, as his reason for tolerating and excusing the murder, that "He's loved of the distracted multitude,/Who like not in their judgement, but their eyes" and who would resent any punishment inflicted on Hamlet.

(iii) To Rosencrantz and Guildenstern, the excuse is made that Hamlet, in madness, killed Polonius; to Laertes, later, the king, in order to direct suspicion away from himself, offers his crown, his life and all that is his if it can be shown that he was in any way responsible for the murder. He also schemes with Laertes to have revenge upon Hamlet.

ACT IV • SCENE 2

Question 1.

How does Hamlet show his contempt in this scene for the king and for his agents, Rosencrantz and Guildenstern? (5-31).

Answer

He accuses his old schoolfellows of flattering and obeying the ruling powers for the sake of rewards and authority. He ridicules their foolishness and condemns them for playing into the hands of the king, who grants them high favors only to enrich himself at their expense. However, he says, the king who can so use them is "a thing of nothing."

ACT IV • SCENE 3

Question 1.

How does the allusion to England made in Scene 3 throw any light upon the date of the events related in the play?

Answer

We have no means of definitely fixing the period of the action of the play, but the reference indicates some date in the eleventh century. England was under the rule of the Northmen from 1017 to 1042, but continued to pay tribute to the Danes at least as late as 1069.

Question 2.

How do you account for Hamlet's displaying his madness before the king in Scene 3, whereas he previously had revealed his "antic disposition" only to Polonius, Ophelia, and Rosencrantz and Guildenstern.

Answer

Shakespeare works up from the lesser characters to Claudius — a natural development of the drama. Hamlet is now prepared to take on directly his "mighty opposite."

Question 3.

By whom, to whom and in what connection is the following passage spoken?

> I see a cherub that sees them.

Answer

After the death of Polonius, the king informs Hamlet of his intention to send him to England for his "especial safety":

> The bark is ready and the wind at help,
> The associates tend, and everything is bent
> For England.

Hamlet, although previously aware of the king's plan, pretends surprise but calmly accepts the order and, as on a former occasion, "with gentle and unforced accord," meekly submits to the king's will. "Good" is his only comment, to which the king replies, "So is it, if thou knew'st our purposes." "I see a cherub that sees them," says Hamlet, thereby implying, heaven knows the king's plans, and that Hamlet resigns himself into the hands of God.

ACT IV • SCENE 4

Question 1.

Illustrate the ambition and energy of Fortinbras.

Answer

In the first and second acts of the play, we heard of young Fortinbras, impatient under his enforced inaction and anxious to redeem the land lost by his father to Denmark. He was prevented from carrying out his greater enterprise. Now we meet him at the head of his band of soldiers, going to expose his own life and the lives of his men "to gain a little patch of ground that hath in it no profit but the name." Hamlet feels the force of this example and eloquently acknowledges the spirit and ambition of the young Norwegian prince.

Question 2.

How does Fortinbras differ in nature from Hamlet?

What effect has the meeting of Hamlet and Fortinbras' army on the former?

Answer

Fortinbras is more impulsive than Hamlet and he is also a man of action. The meeting inspires Hamlet's thoughts in his fourth soliloquy, in which he again analyzes his own uncertain nature.

Question 3.

List several occasions upon which fresh causes arise to spur Hamlet's vengeance.

Answer

Occasions calculated to "spur [his] dull revenge" are (1) the recitation of the player (Act II, Scene 2); (2) the success of "The Mouse-trap" (Act III, Scene 2); (3) the reappearance of the ghost in his mother's chamber (Act III, Scene 4); (4) the news that he is to be sent to England (Act III, Scene 4); (5) the meeting with Fortinbras' army.

ACT IV • SCENE 5

Question 1.

What are the chief points of difference between Ophelia's madness and Hamlet's assumed madness?

Answer

There is all the difference between feigned and real madness, between the purposeful acting of a great intellect and the helpless acts and speeches of a weak, unhinged mind. Hamlet, when he wishes, shows a power of mind superior to that of any other character in the play. Ophelia's insanity is without a break until her death.

Question 2.

What is the cause of Ophelia's insanity?

Answer

"Conceit upon her father," says the king, but this is not the only cause. Allusions to love and lovers show the deep effect on her mind of Hamlet's desertion. The terrible shock to her spirit, caused by her father's death, is only the final act of a tragedy that has already been in progress.

Question 3.

When sorrows come, they come not single spies,
But in battalions!
Expand on the king's statement.

Answer

Polonius has been killed, Hamlet has been sent to England, the people are disturbed and Ophelia is mad. Laertes, back from France, is causing trouble.

Question 4.

Whom does Laertes suspect of being responsible for his father's death?

Answer

That he suspects the king of murder is evident from his violent actions and words, and from the explanations made by both the king and queen. See especially Act IV, Scene 2, 103, 110, 115, 200-4.

Question 5.

Contrast the behavior of Laertes with that of Hamlet at a similar crisis.

Answer

Laertes, in pursuit of vengeance, overcomes every obstacle. Though not an heir to the throne, as Hamlet is, he raises "a rebellion which looks giant-like." Hamlet allows himself to be the victim of circumstances and drifts aimlessly from one event to another. Laertes' passion is sustained until his purpose is achieved; Hamlet is passionate only when enraged for the moment, and then he becomes as "patient as the female dove." Laertes uses his means so well that they "go far with little"; Hamlet, with his enemy within his grasp, hesitates and will not act. The strong-willed Laertes, unafraid of any future world, will "dare damnation" and kill his father's murderer "i' the church," if need be. Hamlet's power of action is lost in the energy of decision, and his "native hue of resolution" is "sicklied o'er with the pale cast of thought."

Question 6.

To which character does Ophelia give each flower?

Answer

Rosemary, for remembrance, is probably given to Laertes; the pansies, for thoughts, to Claudius; fennel, for flattery, probably to Claudius; columbine, for unfaithfulness in marriage, to Gertrude; rue, for repentance, likely to Gertrude; the violet, for loyalty, to Horatio; the daisy, for deceit, to Claudius.

ACT IV • SCENE 6

Question 1.

What is the purpose of this brief scene?

Answer

This scene, in which Horatio receives and reads Hamlet's letter, serves to inform the audience of the prince's progress. Claudius has arranged to have Hamlet killed upon his arrival in England with Rosencrantz and Guildenstern. Ironically, Claudius has just finished assuring Laertes, in Act IV, Scene 5, that "the great axe" is about to fall on Hamlet. In Scene 6, however, we learn that fate has favored Hamlet and we eagerly anticipate Claudius' reaction to this turn of events.

ACT IV • SCENE 7

Question 1.

Show that Laertes is a man of honor only in name, not in deed.

Answer

Not only does Laertes readily fall in with the king's dishonorable suggestions that he should choose "a sword unbated," but, in order to make victory and vengeance doubly sure, he further stains his knightly honor by tipping this sword with poison. He shows a contrast to his careless antagonist, who, "most generous and free from all contriving, will not peruse the foils."

Question 2.

What excuses does Claudius give for not having seized Hamlet?

Answer

He gives two special reasons: "The queen, his mother, lives almost by his looks . . ."; and he thinks it undesirable to take an open stand against Hamlet because of what the public would think.

Question 3.

What is the nature of the plot hatched by Claudius and Laertes? How is such a plot typical of Claudius? How do you explain Laertes' agreeing to it?

Answer

They plot to use poison on the unfoiled rapier and poison in the drink. Their scheme is devious and deceitful, and so is typical of Claudius. Laertes agrees to this plan because he is impulsive and very upset over his father's murder, Ophelia's death and the shortened rites of her funeral.

Question 4.

How are the arrival of Hamlet's letter and the death of Ophelia timed right dramatically?

Answer

Hamlet's letter comes just as the king has Laertes enraged against the prince. Ophelia's death assures Claudius that Laertes will carry out the revenge plan.

Question 5.

Give instances from this act of the use of rhyme. For what purpose is it used?

Answer

In Act IV, Scene 1, 44-5, Scene 3, 68-9, Scene 4, 65-6 and, perhaps, Scene 5, 204-5, a rhyming couplet is used to mark the end of a scene. In Act IV, Scene 5, 19-20, the couplet expresses a general truth or maxim.

Question 8.

Comment on the use of prose in this act.

Answer

Note that Hamlet always uses prose when feigning madness and that the king, in Scene 4, likewise uses prose, or short broken lines, but returns to blank verse as soon as Hamlet leaves the stage. Ophelia, in her madness, speaks in prose when she is not singing snatches of song. Scene 6, except for the last three lines, is all in prose, the usual language of servants (sailors) and the invariable medium for letters. See also Act IV, Scene 7, 43-7.

ACT V • SCENE 1

Question 1.

Is it good drama to have low-comic characters appearing at this stage of the play?

Answer

Probably yes. The gravediggers are highly amusing in themselves and they provide a period of relief between tense scenes.

Question 2.

Contrast the humor of the two gravediggers when in conversation together with that displayed by the first gravedigger and Hamlet.

Answer

The second gravedigger is only a "straight man" for the first. The humor of Hamlet's talk with the first gravedigger is in the witty repartee.

Question 3.

Show that, after Hamlet's entrance, the gravedigging scene entirely changes in character.

Answer

The conversation of the gravediggers before Hamlet comes upon the scene is mere buffoonery, "but the moment that Hamlet opens his lips," says Knight, "the meditative richness of his mind is poured out upon us, and he grapples with the most familiar and yet the deepest thoughts of human nature, in a style that is sublime from its very obviousness and simplicity." The grotesque becomes secondary to the solemn and philosophical.

Question 4.

How do you account for Laertes' being so ready to fight Hamlet and Hamlet's leaping into the grave and getting involved in a struggle with Laertes?

Answer

Laertes blames Hamlet for his father's death and for his sister's madness. Hamlet, on the other hand, resents Laertes' ranting. It is foreign to his own restrained manner.

Question 5.

Professor Dowden has said, "There is in Hamlet a terrible power of sudden and desperate action." Illustrate this statement from the play.

Answer

That Hamlet, when excited and "desperate with imagination" is capable of sudden and vigorous action and can "do such business as the bitter day would quake to look on" is shown in the several tragic actions that lead to the fatal issues depicted in this act. Hamlet acts decisively in the murder of Polonius, the boarding of the pirate vessel and the unsealing and altering of the orders by which he dooms to death his old school fellows. The stabbing of the king, the snatching of the bowl of poison from the hands of Horatio and the selection of Fortinbras to be his successor are also actions suddenly and energetically performed when, in the last few moments of Hamlet's life, no time is left for meditation or delay.

Question 6.

Describe the entrance of the funeral procession and royal mourners.

Answer

It is early morning in the spring (Act IV, Scene 5, 162-171 and Act IV, Scene 7, 168-169). The churchyard mounds are probably green or bright with flowers. The may and hawthorn trees are in full bloom. The first priest precedes the funeral procession and stands in the threshold of the church to forbid the entrance of Ophelia's coffin. The procession is small, with few mourners. Flowers and sweet herbs are carried before the coffin, while the bell in the church tower tolls. The presence of the king, queen and courtiers, and the rich costumes of their followers, indicate that the dead person "was of some estate."

Question 7.

At what point in the play does Hamlet cease to feign madness?

Answer

From the moment of Hamlet's fight at the grave of Ophelia, he is thoroughly himself. He no longer openly insults the king. His mockery of Osric is not disguised as madness, as it was when he held up Polonius to contempt, for he has now put off the "antic disposition." His behavior toward Laertes is that of a perfect gentleman. He shows an affectionate anxiety with regard to the health of the queen, and, in his last moments, he performs the noblest acts of his life.

ACT V • SCENE 2

Question 1.

Indicate the means by which humor is provided in the meeting between Osric and Hamlet. Is such an interlude of humor warranted at this stage of the play?

Answer

Osric's colorful dress, his exaggerated manners, his affected talk, and Hamlet's and Horatio's amusement at all of these pretensions should be noted. As it provides comic relief, this interlude appropriately comes between Ophelia's funeral and the duel.

Question 2.

Explain, with reference to the context:

There's a divinity that shapes our ends
Rough-hew them how we will

Answer

This is the language into which the thoughts of Hamlet shape themselves as he describes to Horatio all the incidents that preceded the dooming to death of Rosencrantz and Guildenstern. He explains how his action was the result of a sudden impulse. He lay in his cabin, too excited to sleep, rose almost unconsciously from his bed, and rashly — "and praised be rashness for it," says he, for "our indiscretion sometimes serves us well" — he performed the deed that was to save his own life and send his two schoolfellows to their deaths. The lesson to be learned, he says, from the success of his involuntary action is that:

There's a divinity that shapes our ends
Rough-hew them how we will.

Question 3.

What affectations of the day are satirized in Osric?

Answer

The affectations satirized are mainly those extravagances of language that originated in the *Euphues* of John Lyly. The euphuist has a weakness for conceited style, speaks in antithesis, uses fancy similes and enjoys eccentric and tasteless tricks of speech. Osric, with many fantastic expressions, praises the qualities of the knight who has returned from France. Hamlet, in intentionally confused language, mimics Osric's oddities to expose his shallowness and the shallowness of "many more of the same breed that the drossy age dotes on."

It has been suggested by some commentators that Shakespeare intended, not only in this scene, but also in the whole play, to satirize Montaigne and his host of English admirers. The publication in English of Montaigne's *Essays* in 1603 was an important event in the intellectual London world, and there is enough evidence scattered through the play to show that Shakespeare's mind was preoccupied with Montaigne's *Essays* at the time of the writing of the second edition of *Hamlet* (1604).

Question 4.

Upon what grounds does Hamlet justify the murder of Rosencrantz and Guildenstern?

Answer

Just as, after the murder of Polonius, Hamlet felt compelled to reason with his conscience and to console himself with the thought that loving kindness forced him to be cruel, so now he justifies to Horatio his action with regard to his schoolfellows:

> Why man, they did make love to this employment;
> they are not near my conscience.

Again, he regards himself as an instrument of heaven's vengeance. The death of his schoolfellows was the divinely appointed punishment for their "insinuations" – meddling with other people's affairs.

Question 5.

Show how events immediately preceding the climax and the climax itself, make this final scene one of the most stirring in Shakespeare.

Answer

Tension in the selection of the foils, the suspense as to whether Claudius' plot will succeed, the excitement of the duel itself, the surprising death of the queen, the success and, at the same time, the failure of Claudius' plan, Laertes' remorse and revelation of Claudius' treachery, and the deaths of all the principal characters all make for a most exciting scene.

Question 6.

Show that the "towering passion" that Hamlet feels at Ophelia's grave is genuine. What are Hamlet's real sentiments toward Laertes?

Answer

In Act V, Scene 1, 225, Hamlet describes Laertes as "a very noble youth." In this scene, which ends so disastrously to them both, he courts Laertes' "favours," describes him as a gentleman and a brother, and appeals to "his most generous thoughts." His last words to Laertes are a prayer that heaven will forgive the part Laertes took in bringing about his own death.

Question 7.

By what was Hamlet probably motivated in his acceptance of Laertes' challenge?

Answer

In this incident, Shakespeare once more shows how Hamlet allows himself to be influenced and driven to a decision. He accepts the challenge because his self-respect is at stake, and, for appearance's sake, he must remain "constant to his purposes." He confesses his misgivings to Horatio, but he lacks the firmness to act upon his friend's advice to delay the match.

In connection with this incident, a discrepancy may be noticed between two statements in the play. In Act II, Scene 2, Hamlet is made to say that he has "foregone all custom of exercise," yet in Scene 2 of this act, he says that, since Laertes went to France, he (Hamlet) had been in continual practice.

Question 8.

Show that Hamlet, after accepting the challenge, feels a sense of doom.

Answer

Hamlet's sense of doom is revealed in his remark to Horatio, "Thou would'st not think how ill all's here about my heart!" and his fatalism is also apparent in his words, "There is special providence in the fall of a sparrow. If it be now, 'tis not to come; if it be not to come, it will be now; if it be not now, yet it will come. . . . Let be."

Question 9.

"The Hamlet of the play is a heroic, terrible figure." Can you substantiate this description?

Answer

The quotation is from Bradley, who, arguing against the theory of a "sentimental" Hamlet, asks us to "consider the text" and briefly reviews Hamlet's deeds of daring and violence as described in the play: his strong action in the presence of the ghost (Act I, Scene 4, 82-5), his consistently insulting behavior toward the king and Polonius, his killing of the eavesdropping Polonius and sending his "schoolfellows" to their deaths, his storming at Ophelia and speaking "daggers" to his mother, his boarding a pirate ship and his fighting Laertes in the grave. Finally, "the Hamlet of the catastrophe, an omnipotent fate, before whom all the court stands helpless. . . . This man, the Hamlet of the play, is a heroic, terrible figure. He would have been formidable to Othello or Macbeth. If the sentimental Hamlet had crossed him, he would have hurled him from his path with one sweep of his arm."

Question 10.

How does Horatio, even to the end, hold true as a fine, honorable character?

Answer

Horatio is the one to whom Hamlet turns in the end. Hamlet relies on Horatio to explain everything. Horatio would have preferred to die with his friend, but he stays on to do his duty.

Part C: General Review Questions and Answers

Question 1.

To what extent is *Hamlet* based on actual history? What sources did Shakespeare draw upon?

Answer

No actual historical foundation for the story of *Hamlet* has been discovered. But, as the story is found in the pages of the *Historia Danica*, written by the Danish historian, Saxo Grammaticus, it is probable that the tale has some foundation in fact. Saxo Grammaticus lived during the latter part of the twelfth and earlier part of the thirteenth centuries. He wrote his history of *Hamlet*, or *Amleth*, in Latin. It is possible that Shakespeare had read this work, but it is much more probable that he obtained his materials from the French version of Belleforest, who introduced the story into his *Cent Histoires Tragiques.* The story, as told by Belleforest, was also translated into English under the title, *The Historie of Hamblet*. The main points of resemblance between Shakespeare's plot and that of the *Historie* are: the murder of Hamlet's father by his uncle, and the incestuous marriage of the latter with the queen; the feigned madness of Hamlet; the scene in which Hamlet condemns his mother and murders Polonius; his voyage to England, together with his forgery of the letters, resulting in the deaths of the messengers; his return and his revenge. In Belleforest's novel, Hamlet's father is called Horvendile, his uncle is Fengon and his mother is Geruth. The characters of Laertes and Ophelia are altogether absent from the original story, which includes Hamlet's successful elevation to the throne of Denmark and several subsequent adventures that do not concern us here.

There is also supposed to have existed a play about Hamlet as early as 1587. This version may or may not have been a very early production of Shakespeare, but, in any case, there is every reason to believe that he had at least seen it.

Question 2.

What is the date and form of the earliest known edition of the play?

Answer

The earliest known edition of the play was printed in 1603, with this title:

> The Tragicall Historie of Hamlet, Prince of Denmarke, By William Shakespeare. As it hath beene diverse times acted by his Highnesse servants in the Cittie of London: as also in the two Vniversities of Cambridge and Oxford, and elsewhere. At London printed for N.L. and Iohn Trundell, 1603.

In this edition, the First Quarto differs materially from the Second Quarto, which contains the play in the shape in which we now have it. The edition of 1603 contains 32 leaves; that of 1604 contains 50. In the former, there are 2,143 lines; in the latter, 3,719. The Quarto of 1603 has many errors and shows traces of having been hastily printed; the later copy was printed with much more care. In the first edition, the scene with Ophelia (Act III, Scene1) is placed in the second act, Polonius is called Corambis and Reynaldo is Montano. These facts tend to show that the earlier edition was not merely a pirated copy of the complete work. It has been suggested that, in the earlier form, Shakespeare's modification of a still older play on the same subject — supposed to have been printed in 1587 or 1589, but of which no edition is still in existence — had not gone much beyond the second act. Thus, the edition of 1603 contains some of Shakespeare's undoubted work, mixed with a great deal (taken from the older play) that is not his and represents the older play in a transition state. In the Quarto of 1604, we have, for the first time, the *Hamlet* of Shakespeare.

Question 3.

What historical events of Queen Elizabeth's reign may have suggested to Shakespeare the legend from which he derived his play?

Answer

The events that took place in Scotland in 1567, — the murder of Darnley and the marriage of his widow, Mary Stuart, with Lord Bothwell — may have suggested the theme of *Hamlet* to the poet's mind. The incident of Fortinbras' expedition may have been suggested by one of Sir Walter Raleigh's hazardous enterprises.

Question 4.

What were the steps by which Hamlet became satisfied that Claudius was his father's murderer? Have the spectators any information that is withheld from Hamlet?

Answer

A vague suspicion of "foul play" seems to have occurred to Hamlet during Horatio's speech. (Act I, Scene 2). The direct revelation made by the ghost convinces him, for the time being, of the "most foul, strange, and unnatural murder." Then Hamlet forms his resolution. But, with Hamlet, much happens between deciding his purpose and the first motion toward its achievement. During the interval of a few weeks, his indecision leads to doubt, and he requires more absolute proof. This he obtains by means of the play, *The Murder of Gonzago* (Act III, Scene 2), with his additions. Hamlet's test succeeds; now he will "take the ghost's word for a thousand pound." Furthermore, he now has a witness to the king's guilt — his calm, self-possessed friend, Horatio, "who is not passion's slave."

Other evidence of Claudius' guilt thrusts itself upon the procrastinating, reluctant hero during the second visitation of the ghost (Act III, Scene 4), which comes to remind Hamlet of his "almost blunted purpose," and in the king's excessive anxiety to send the prince, "with fiery quickness," to England. When Hamlet discovers by reading the sealed communiqué that the king has "thrown out his angle" for his life, the proof of the king's guilt can go no further. "Is't not perfect conscience," asks Hamlet, "to quit him with this arm?/And is't not to be damn'd to let this canker of our nature come in further evil?" (Act V, Scene 2).

The spectators do possess information that is withheld from Hamlet. In Act III, Scene 1, the king's conscience is troubled, and he displays to the audience the spectacle of a man suffering from guilt and burdened by his crime. When, after "The Mouse-trap," the king attempts to make his peace with heaven, the audience hears his self-condemning words:

O, my offence is rank: it smells to heaven;
It hath the primal eldest curse upon't,
A brother's murder.

Then the king gives his reason for his inability to pray:

Since I am still possess'd
Of those effects for which I did the murder,
My crown, mine own ambition, and my queen.

Question 5.

(i) Show why the general situation presented in Act I causes Hamlet, at the close of this act, to exclaim:

The time is out of joint; O cursed spite,
That ever I was born to set it right!

(ii) Indicate the significance of these words with regard to Hamlet's further part in the play.

Answer

(i) As the play opens, one knows that all is not well in Denmark. The preparation for the expected battle with Fortinbras is not the only reason that "the time is out of joint." Even the guards realize that the appearance of the ghost of the late king is a strange and ominous sign. The marriage of the queen to her husband's brother so soon after her husband's death seems unusual; mourning for only two months would be uncustomary. The smooth-talking, jovial king, who is crowned instead of the former king's popular son further complicates matters in the kingdom. The fact that Hamlet, although mourning deeply for his father's death and his mother's action, cannot speak his feelings also seems strange. When Hamlet hears of his father's ghost, he remarks:

My father's spirit in arms! all is not well;
I doubt some foul play.

Thus, when he hears that his suspicions regarding Claudius' guilt are proved true, events really seem to be "out of joint." The murder of a brother is a despicable crime, and, when it is committed something is wrong with civilization. Although Hamlet wants desperately to avenge his father's foul and most unnatural murder," he realizes that he is hampered by many things. He cannot kill his lawful king without stirring up the people. His father's ghost ordered him,

> Taint not thy mind, nor let thy soul contrive
> Against thy mother aught.

When the first impulsive thought of revenge has passed, Hamlet becomes the careful and perhaps lazy person his habit has created. Thus, on more reflection, it seems to Hamlet that some power has chosen him to correct the rottenness in the state, and this responsibility weighs heavily on him.

(ii) Although these words indicate Hamlet's willingness to give up easily, later he does try to achieve his purpose, but his thoughts render him inactive. He decides that he needs proof that the ghost is not the devil, so he devises a clever play to test the ghost's accusation. This action proves Claudius' guilt. Just as Hamlet is ready to "drink hot blood," he lets his thoughts talk him out of killing Claudius while the king prays. If Hamlet had been of a firm mind to kill his uncle, he could have prevented his own ultimate death. Instead, his impetuosity kills Polonius and places Hamlet in Claudius' hands. On the way to England, having discovered the real reason for the trip, Hamlet again acts purposefully by forging new orders and abandoning the ship during an attack. However, Claudius still is able to plan Hamlet's death in a duel. Hamlet does kill Claudius, but his revenge comes too late to save himself and his mother. Had he not delayed because of self-pity and his inability to act, this would not have been a tragic play.

Question 6.

Select three scenes in which Hamlet assumes an "antic disposition." Describe briefly the actual mood or emotion that seems to lie behind this disguise in each case, supporting your opinion with details from the scene.

Answer

Hamlet puts on an antic disposition in front of Polonius when the lord chamberlain meets the prince while he is reading. Hamlet is in a sarcastic mood when he calls Polonius a "fishmonger." When Polonius asks him what he is reading, Hamlet replies: "Words, words, words." Thus, Hamlet is scornful and impatient in his conversation with Polonius.

Hamlet also puts on an antic disposition with Ophelia after the "To be or not to be" soliloquy. Here, his mood is one of resentment and bitterness. Hamlet is full of resentment when he tells Ophelia, "I loved you once" and then contradicts himself with "I loved you not." He is bitter when he says: "Get thee to a nunnery." He tells her that, if she has to marry, she should marry a fool, for wise men know what fools women make of them.

Hamlet behaves strangely with Rosencrantz and Guildenstern when they come to ask him for Polonius' body. Here, he is sarcastic and bitter to his former friends. He tells them that they are like sponges, soaking up the king's pleasure. Hamlet also compares them to nuts that the king puts at the back of his mouth and eats when he no longer needs them.

Question 7.

Select two major situations in which Hamlet, without his "antic disposition," encounters an inferior, or group of inferiors. Describe a particular characteristic that he displays in each case.

Answer

In the graveyard scene, Hamlet reveals a pleasing personality in his conversation with the gravedigger. He does not treat the common people as inferiors. He joins in the literal quibbling of the gravedigger, without any feeling of superiority.

When the travelling players arrive, Hamlet is enthusiastic, welcoming them heartily and deriving pleasure from their wonderful talents. He reveals his respect for the actors and their profession in his advice to them and in his familiarity with Hecuba's speech.

Question 8.

Describe briefly two important examples of dramatic irony, in each case explaining the source of the ironic effect.

Answer

Dramatic irony may be defined as an effect produced when characters speak, or act, in ignorance of the full significance of what they say or do, while the audience is aware of that significance and, hence, of the characters' ignorance. Dramatic irony is shown, in a delayed form, in Lady Macbeth's case when she says, "A little water clears us of this deed." The irony is not complete until the sleepwalking scene, when it becomes evident that she cannot wash herself clean of the stains of guilt.

Dramatic irony is apparent in *Hamlet* when Claudius and Laertes seek to destroy Hamlet with a poisoned sword, but become victims of their own treachery. This type of dramatic irony, involving a reversal of the situation intended, is known as *peripeteia*.

A second example of dramatic irony in *Hamlet* occurs when "divinity" is associated with a "mildewed ear" (obviously referring to Claudius) in Act 4, Scene 5. When Claudius states,

> There's such divinity doth hedge a king,
> That treason can but peep to what it would,
> Acts little of his will,

it seems that he has, for the moment, forgotten the act of treachery without which he would not have become king. The irony, in this case, lies in his forgetfulness or disregard of his own situation in making a general statement.

Question 9.

Locate the turning point of the play. Justify your choice by relating it to three subsequent major developments.

Answer

The turning point of the play occurs during the "Mouse-trap" scene, when King Claudius rises and shouts, "Lights, Light, light!" and then leaves. From here on, Claudius becomes the aggressor in the conflict between him and Hamlet.

Having proved that the ghost is really that of his father and that Claudius is indeed the murderer, Hamlet becomes tense and excited. He goes to see his mother, planning to "speak daggers but use none." In this state of mind, immediately after the success of his plot carried out in the play scene, Hamlet acts swiftly when Polonius cries out while hiding behind a curtain in the queen's room. Hamlet kills him and asks, "Is it the king?" This act now places Hamlet in the same position that Claudius is in. That is, as Hamlet must avenge his father's death, so must Laertes now kill Hamlet to avenge Polonius' death.

The king quickly realizes that Hamlet is a threat to his safety. As a direct result of the play scene, he knows that Hamlet has somehow discovered that he, Claudius, murdered King Hamlet. Therefore, Claudius plans to get rid of Hamlet by sending him to England with Rosencrantz and Guildenstern, who will carry an order for Hamlet's death. Hamlet's discovery of this plot reveals to him the treachery of Claudius and results in the deaths of Hamlet's two "friends."

When Claudius learns that Hamlet has escaped the plot, he hatches another plan to bring about Hamlet's death. Now, Claudius has Laertes to help him kill Hamlet, because Laertes greatly desires to avenge the death of Polonius. Claudius proposes a duel in which Laertes will have an unblunted sword, and Laertes plans to poison the tip. The King also plans to poison a drink of wine for Hamlet. This new plot leads to the tragedy in the last scene. Gertrude drinks the poisoned wine, both Hamlet and Laertes are poisoned by the sword, and Claudius is killed by Hamlet.

Question 10.

Select a scene of fairly broad comedy, and explain one of its important dramatic functions.

Answer

The gravedigger scene (Act V, Scene 1) provides the most humor in the play. In this scene, the first and second gravediggers provide comic relief with their riddles, misquoted Latin and general good humor.

In Act IV, Scene 7, the queen returns to Laertes and Claudius, who have just finished plotting Hamlet's murder, and tells of Ophelia's drowning. This scene is one of high tension and drama. The gravedigger scene gives welcome relief after the audience's excitement has reached a peak. The following part of the play, in which Hamlet battles with Laertes over Ophelia's dead body, is also one of high drama. If it followed directly after Ophelia's death, the tension would be unbearable, and the audience would lose contact with the conflict.

The gravedigger scene gives the audience a chance to relax and laugh (something rarely possible throughout this play), preparing for the following tension. The humor in the scene is provided by the setting, a graveyard, and the merriment of the gravediggers as they dig and toss out old bones "like loggats." They try to act refined by using such terms as "se offendando" for "se defendendo." The two riddles, although grim and, thus, tying in with the tone of the play, provide humor and relief. One gravedigger asks, "Who builds strongest?" His companion answers, "The gallows-maker, for his house outlasts a thousand tents." This sort of humor allows for dramatic relief.

Question 11.

Answer the following questions on Hamlet's soliloquy, beginning "O what a rogue and peasant slave am I." (Act II, Scene 2, 553-611)

(i) Paraphrase the ideas presented in it.
(ii) Show its dramatic significance.
(iii) Discuss its poetic merits.

Answer

(i) How feeble, how poverty-stricken I am. Why, even this poor actor can summon up more force, more feeling, when taking a dramatic part, than I can raise when confronted, as I am, with a problem in real life. What would this actor do in my place? Would he not be able to put on a show that would make everybody think? Of course he would. Yet I can do and say nothing — no, not even to avenge my own father's damnable murder. Is it cowardice in me? It may be that I do lack courage — otherwise would I not have slain Claudius long ago? Claudius, that treacherous, ruthless, unnatural knave! — But what am I doing? Merely talking, when actions are needed. Just a minute: I have an idea! I will have these actors perform a play before my uncle, in which his murder of my father shall be reflected. While he watches this play, I shall observe his reactions closely. If he is at all upset, I shall know that he is guilty. By this means, I can test the truth of the ghost's message to me. I need concrete, realistic evidence, not just the unconfirmed testimony of a ghost. The play's the thing with which I shall trap the king's conscience.

(ii) The dramatic significance of this soliloquy is that it shows Hamlet is a cautious man who needs evidence upon which to base his actions. He plans to obtain psychological evidence before, presumably, carrying out his revenge. His subtle plan is entirely characteristic of his own deep, rich nature. Thus, this soliloquy adds to the complication, while further revealing character and plot.

(iii) Poetic merits.

This soliloquy is in iambic pentameter, blank (unrhymed) verse. Its language is personal and direct, giving an effect of spontaneity. The poetic merits are many and varied, but two stand out: the effective imagery ("murder, though it hath no tongue, will speak/With most miraculous organ") in which the crime, murder, is personified, and alliteration of the *m* sounds sustains the effect; and the dramatic intermingling of the two voices of Hamlet, that of the calm, reasonable aristocrat (as in "O, what a rogue and peasant slave am I!") contrasted with that of the passionate, disturbed man (as in "this slave's offal"). Hamlet realizes that he has been speaking out of character when he accuses himself of having had to

> unpack my heart with words,
> And fall a cursing, like a very drab.
> A scullion.

This mixing of courtly vocabulary with household cursing is an effective poetic device because it reveals Hamlet's mind working at two levels when trying to resolve his tragic conflict.

Question 12.

Referring to three different scenes of *Hamlet*, either support or oppose the following statement, made by Hamlet to Laertes.

His madness is poor Hamlet's enemy.

Answer

Hamlet, speaking of himself in Act V, Scene 2, seeks to excuse himself to Laertes for having killed Polonius.

First, we must establish whether Hamlet was "mad" when he killed Polonius. That slaying occurred in the queen's bedroom, in Act III, Scene 4, at a time when Hamlet was condemning his mother. His speech was logical and extremely highminded. In lines 170-171, he stated:

For this same lord,
[Pointing to the body of Polonius]
I do repent:

Hamlet has mistaken Polonius for his "better" — that is, Claudius. Therefore, it seems clear that Hamlet's madness did not cause the death of Polonius. The death was caused by ironic miscalculation on Hamlet's part. Because Hamlet's action alienated Laertes, the deed itself was "poor Hamlet's enemy." But, again, it was not madness, but the rashness of the killing, that created this conflict between Laertes and Hamlet.

We must now question whether "madness" was ever one of Hamlet's characteristics. In Act I, Scene 5, Hamlet confided to Horatio that he would "put an antic disposition on" (behave fantastically to divert suspicion from his true purpose), but we are made to realize that Hamlet intended to be in control of this disposition.

In his subsequent encounters with the gentle Ophelia, however, Hamlet behaved with uncharacteristic ruthlessness, brutality and vulgarity. Was this true madness? Had he allowed the antic disposition to master him? Not necessarily. He could not afford to trust Ophelia and he did not know who might be eavesdropping on their private conversations.

Therefore, the quotation would seem to be figurative, rather than strictly literal in meaning. It represents an artificial attempt by Hamlet to talk himself out of a rather difficult situation and to talk himself back into the good graces of Laertes.

Question 13.

"The chief character in this tragedy is progressively isolated, cut off more and more from normal relationships with relatives, friends, associates, and the public."

(i) Describe three significant incidents from various parts of the play to demonstrate whether this statement is true of Hamlet.

(ii) Describe, in a sentence or two, three different attempts made by other characters to promote "normal relationships" with Hamlet.

Answer

(i) Hamlet was cut off from his father by the sudden death of the king. After encountering his father's ghost, Hamlet assumes an "antic disposition" that alienates him from Ophelia and probably contributes to her madness and death. His mother's weakness of character and her immorality (as Hamlet considered her new marriage) alienated mother and son, although Hamlet made a heroic, but only partially successful, effort to reform his mother and end their alienation in Act III, Scene 4. By accidentally killing Polonius, Hamlet cut himself off from that doubtful source of consolation and advice. His relation with Claudius, never close, was based on increasing mutual suspicion and dislike, moderated by formal good manners. Rosencrantz and Guildenstern soon lose Hamlet's respect and friendship by their eagerness to betray him. Hamlet forfeits Laertes' friendship by killing Polonius. He only succeeds in recovering Laertes' goodwill just before the fencing match. Thus, Hamlet does become isolated from everybody except his friend, Horatio.

(ii) In different, characteristic ways, three attempts were made by minor characters to promote "normal relationships" with Hamlet. Polonius, believing Hamlet to be mad with love for Ophelia, in Act II, Scene 2, questions him gently:

> O, give me leave, how does my good lord Hamlet?

Polonius seems to show his genuine concern later, in the same conversation, by asking directly:

> What is the matter, my lord?

But Hamlet misinterprets this question, all Polonius meant was, "What are you reading?"

A second attempt to promote "normal relationships" is made by his school acquaintances and apparent friends, Rosencrantz and Guildenstern, later in Act II, Scene 2, beginning with the overenthusiastic and ironic greeting, "God save you, sir!"

A third attempt is made by Ophelia, in Act III, Scene 1, when she opens a conversation with Hamlet with the sympathetic question,

> Good my lord,
> How does your honour for this many a day?

Hamlet, in accordance with the demands of the "antic disposition" that he had previously decided to assume, replies to all these attempts with evasive tactics. Puns, and other conscious misunderstandings dominate his speeches. Such tactics are contrary to the spirit of the attempts of others to promote "normal relationships."

Question 14.

"Our interest in the chief person in the tragedy is sustained by repeated evidences of his good qualities."

Use three significant incidents or situations from various parts of *Hamlet* to show how each reveals both a good quality and a less admirable quality of Hamlet.

Answer

In Act II, Scene 2, Hamlet spontaneously conceives the idea of using a play to trap the conscience of a king. This plan shows Hamlet's instinctive feeling for theatrical tricks and a certain degree of ingenuity. It also shows his burning desire to be certain of Claudius' guilt. These two good qualities are offset, however, by Hamlet's self-doubt and his passionate and self-destructive mockery.

In Act III, Scene 1, the soliloquy "To be, or not to be" raises the problem of Hamlet's committing suicide because he cannot resolve the conflicts that trouble him. A certain measure of self-criticism and philosophic introspection is good, but Hamlet carries these qualities to the point where they become emotionally destructive and almost lead to suicide. Thus, a good quality becomes bad by being carried to extremes.

In Act V, Scene 2, Hamlet acknowledges that he has wronged Laertes by killing Polonius, and immediately asks his pardon. The frank, open manner with which Hamlet does this is a credit to him. There is impetuosity here (as there was in the spur-of-the-moment slaying of the old courtier that must have brought an instant response from the even more impetuous Laertes. However, this momentary impetuosity in Hamlet is contradicted by his prevailing uncertainty, seen throughout the play.

Question 15.

Describe two qualities of Hamlet that he reveals only to Horatio.

Answer

In Act V, Scene 1, the gravedigger scene, Hamlet reveals to Horatio a detached philosophical outlook that he reveals to nobody else in the play. He has seen the gravedigger toss up a skull and, talking to Horatio, reveals his philosophy of life and death. "Alas, poor Yorick. I knew him well, Horatio — a fellow of infinite jest." Hamlet tells Horatio how touched he is by the fact that "those lips which so oft I kissed" are now gone. We see Hamlet as a man whose thoughts have profound roots. He philosophizes to Horatio on the uselessness of ambition, stating that one could trace the career of Alexander the Great to the point where his dust is used to plug a "bunghole."

In Act III, Scene 2, Hamlet reveals to Horatio the sort of ideal man he would like to be. He says he admires Horatio for the traits that he finds noble in men. He shows us exactly how he wishes his character had developed. He says, "Give me the man who is not passion's slave." He admires people who "take Fortune's buffets and rewards with equal thanks." When he says that he admires men such as Horatio, in whom "passion and judgment are so well commingled," he gives us his idea of perfection. This statement provides an indication of what Hamlet would like to be, compared to what he is.

Question 16.

Using clear references to a single scene in the latter part of the play, describe two significant changes that have been brought about in the character of Hamlet and show how these changes are revealed to the audience.

Answer

In Act V, Hamlet becomes less inactive than formerly, though with tragic consequences. Thus, in Scene 1, Hamlet leaps into Ophelia's open grave and fights with Laertes, afterward declaring his love for the dead girl in extravagant and deliberately rhetorical terms:

> forty thousand brothers
> Could not, with all their quantity of love,
> Make up my sum.

This ranting shows how much Hamlet has parted from his early, reserved manner. He speaks more like a commoner than a nobleman at this moment.

Secondly, he addresses Laertes directly, with a blunt command followed by a question:

> Hear you, sir:
> What is the reason that you use me thus?
> I loved you ever: but it is no matter . . .

There is, in this speech, a new consciousness of power that contrasts with Hamlet's previous timidity.

Question 17.

Describe three distinctive qualities of Hamlet's character and show how each quality affects the tragic development of the play.

Answer

One distinctive quality of Hamlet's character is his habit of introspection, revealed in his philosophic soliloquies. This habit causes Hamlet to suffer at the thought of his mother's remarriage, within such a brief time, to such a man as Claudius. It is also the cause of his doubt concerning

Claudius' guilt and of the delay in executing vengeance.

The second of Hamlet's distinctive qualities is his sophistication and refinement, attributes that lead him to express great interest in the activities of the players when they arrive at the castle. He immediately perceives how, with the play-within-the-play, he might prove the guilt of Claudius. His cleverness in devising "The Mouse-trap" and in having it performed at the correct instant are revealed in Act II, Scene 2.

The third distinctive quality of Hamlet might be either his friendliness (shown in his relations with Horatio and, at the outset, with Rosencrantz and Guildenstern) or his bitter sarcasm, shown when he speaks of those whom he considers untrustworthy. (Act V, Scene 1, 298; Act V, Scene 2, 233)

Question 18.

Discuss briefly, using appropriate references, the dramatic value of the part taken in the play by Laertes.

Answer

The character of Laertes is directly opposite to that of Hamlet. The former is impulsive, while the latter is uncertain.

> The ocean . . .
> Eats not the flats with more impetuous haste
> Than young Laertes . . .
> (Act IV, Scene 5, 85-7)

Laertes is less refined and considerably wilder than Hamlet. He does not hesitate to set out to punish the man who killed his father and contributed to his sister's madness and suicide. Therefore, Laertes shows how a man with a very different character from Hamlet's reacts when he finds himself in virtually the same position as Hamlet. Shakespeare obviously intended to use Laertes as a foil to Hamlet. All of Hamlet's richness and complexity stand out when he is compared to Laertes.

Question 19.

Write short notes on the parts of Rosencrantz and Guildenstern, Osric and the gravediggers.

Answer

Rosencrantz and Guildenstern are important as a type, rather than from any actions or speeches of their own. They represent fawning, flattering courtiers that "soak up the king's countenance, his rewards, his authorities" and are ready for any immoral and despicable work in his service. These characters may be supposed to have had a good education — they were Hamlet's schoolfellows — and to have been well acquainted with the arts and accomplishments of conventional society. They are a team, each deriving support and confidence from the presence of the other. Lacking originality, they form their opinions upon all subjects in accordance with the fashion of the day and are satisfied if they can get "the tune of the time and outward habit of encounter." Their knowledge is superficial and their intelligence mediocre, so that they are easily outwitted by Hamlet in any argument. They are not great criminals, having neither initiative nor courage, acuteness of judgment or shrewdness. They are fools, rather than knaves. Although they meet with a severer punishment than they deserve, we feel no pity for them.

Osric is a fashionable gentleman of the court. He owns much fertile land and, therefore, stands high in the king's favor. He is a friend of Laertes, whose qualities he admires and for whom he acts as second in the duel. His language is affected. He deals in high-flown compliments and makes a great show of politeness. When his shallowness and superficiality are exposed by Hamlet, he either does not, or will not, perceive the satire of which he is the object. There is some doubt as to whether he is aware of the treachery against Hamlet's life, but we cannot fail to regard with some suspicion the man who gives the contestants their foils and to whom Laertes, when wounded with the poisoned sword, exclaims,

> Why, as a woodcock to mine own springe, Osric,
> I am justly killed with mine own treachery.

The gravediggers are introduced discussing the legality of Ophelia's burial in holy ground. On this, as on other topics, they express their opinions with almost socialistic freedom. This tendency toward socialism is perceived by Hamlet, who says, "the age is grown so picked that the toe of the peasant comes so near the heel of the courtier, he galls his kibe." These gravediggers have lost all feeling for their business and they sing and crack jokes as though gravedigging were the pleasantest trade on earth. The first gravedigger seeks to show his cleverness and ingenuity in words; he has caught the wit of the age and can reason and philosophize about philosophers with the prince.

Question 20.

Describe the conduct of Laertes after his return from France and show how Shakespeare makes him a foil to Hamlet.

Answer

Laertes, on hearing of his father's death, returns in secret from Paris,

> Feeds on his wonder, keeps himself in clouds,
> And wants not buzzers to infect his ear
> With pestilent speeches of his father's death.

Rumor acquainted him with the suspicious circumstances surrounding the death of Polonius — his funeral unmarked by ceremonial rites, the absence of "formal ostentation" and the suddenness with which the end came. Such neglect in the case of a high officer of state, casts suspicion on the king. Laertes does not wait for proof but, with impetuous haste, like "The ocean, overpeering of his list," he is anxious for his revenge. He rushes madly into the king's presence, allowing no earthly obstacle to stop him. He even dares damnation in order that he may have revenge for the death of his father. His passion, unlike that of Hamlet, is sustained until his enemy is defeated. He does not falter during the fencing match, and, while confessing that "it is almost against his conscience," he deals the fatal blow that avenges his father's death.

In all his actions, he presents a forcible contrast to the indecisive prince. Hamlet, with the most convincing proof of Claudius' guilt, allows time to slip away in purposeless speculation, being distracted from action by "some craven scruple of thinking too precisely on the event." Laertes leaves himself no time for thought; Hamlet's time is too much taken up with thought to allow him to act. Opportunity thrusts itself in Hamlet's way, yet he will not take advantage of it. Conscience makes a coward of him, and his "native hue of resolution" is "sicklied o'er with the pale cast of thought." Laertes does not worry about staining his honor by poisoning his weapon; Hamlet has such a free and generous nature that he does not so much as glance at the foils. With Hamlet, revenge has become a religious duty, imposed upon him by a spirit from another world; with Laertes it is a matter of honor. Not only was Hamlet's father murdered in cold blood, but his mother's name was stained and his own rights of succession were forfeited. Polonius' death, however, was accidentally brought about in a fit of passion by a man who immediately repented and grieved for what he had done. There is a great contrast between the murdered fathers. King Hamlet was:

A combination and a form indeed,
Where every god did seem to set his seal
To give the world assurance of a man.

Polonius, however, was "a tedious old fool," a ridiculous, talkative, prying and smug old man.

Question 21.

Show how Hamlet is excitable, affectionate, melancholy, sarcastic and refined.

Answer

Excitable: When the ghost appears to Hamlet, his "fate cries out:"

And makes each petty artery in this body
As hardy as the Nemean lion's nerve.

The ghost finds him "apt," and, indeed, at that moment, "desperate with imagination," he longs to seek his revenge:

With wings as swift
As meditation, or the thoughts of love.

He is still under the influence of excitement produced by his interview with the ghost when he decides to assume an antic disposition.

After "The Mouse-trap" has been sprung, in "the very witching time of the night," he can:

Drink hot blood,
And do such bitter business as the day
Would quake to look upon.

In such a mood, he cruelly torments his mother and rashly murders Polonius, mistaking him for the king. His excitable nature is roused to passion, on other occasions, by the player's speech, by the example of Fortinbras and by the sight of Laertes' grief at Ophelia's grave. On this last occasion, Hamlet falls into uncontrollable rage:

Woo't weep? woo't fight? woo't fast? woo't tear
  thyself?
Woo't drink up eisel? — eat a crocodile
I'll do't,

he exclaims, and his actions show that the violence of his emotion has in it something dangerous. But his passion is as short-lived as it is violent. To Horatio, he repents and promises to make amends to Laertes. All his sudden actions — the dooming to death of his schoolfellows, the murder of the king, the snatching of the bowl of poison from Horatio — are performed upon the impulse of the moment and in sudden inspirations of excited feelings.

Affectionate: He respected, admired and loved his father, whom he describes as his "dear murthered father" and of whom he says:

He was a man, take him for all in all;
I shall not look upon his like again.

Hamlet loved Ophelia, and she responded with gentle, clinging affection. At her graveside, in passionate words, he exclaims:

Forty thousand brothers
Could not, with all their quantity of love,
Make up my sum.

But his affection for Horatio is more deep-seated. In his friend's nature, he finds something that makes up for his own deficiencies. In Horatio, he finds relief from his sense of loneliness. Of him, he says:

Since my dear soul was mistress of my choice,
And could of men distinguish, her election
Hath sealed thee for herself.

Hamlet's gentle nature feels sympathy even for Laertes in his grief.

Melancholy: He first appears in the drama dressed in mourning, with "dejected 'haviour of the visage," the clouds still hanging on him. The queen urges him:

Do not for ever with thy vailed lids
Seek for thy noble father in the dust.

In his first soliloquy, he utters the bitter words:

O that this too too sullied flesh would melt,
Thaw, and resolve itself into a dew!

He regards the world as a prison; the earth as "an unweeded garden," "a sterile promontory," the sky as "a foul and pestilent congregation of vapours." He loses all his joy and "walks for hours together" in the palace hall. "Look where sadly the poor wretch comes reading," says the queen on one occasion. After the player's recitation, Hamlet refers to his own melancholy mood and imagines that he may have been all along tricked by the devil, who:

Out of my weakness and my melancholy,
As he is very potent with such spirits,
Abuses me to damn me.

He seems to dwell on thoughts of death and suicide (Act III,

Scene 1, 56-67). From Hamlet's interview with Ophelia, the king concludes that:

> There's something in his soul
> O'er which his melancholy sits on brood.

All Hamlet's fits of impulsive action are followed by periods of melancholy and despair. After his first interview with the ghost, he curses his fate; after the death of Polonius, he weeps; after his passionate scene with Laertes, his silence "sit[s], drooping." In the last act, his conversation with Laertes and his solemn reflections in the graveyard scene show the melancholy that has now become habitual with him.

Sarcastic: Hamlet makes many sarcastic images, comparisons and allusions in his varying moods. At times, his sarcasm is witty and humorous, as when he fools Polonius (Act II, Scene 2; Act III, Scene 2), ridicules the courtiers (Act II, Scene 2; Act IV, Scene 2), indulges in trifling conversation with Ophelia (Act III, Scene 2), and satirizes the follies of "this drossy age" in Osric (Act V, Scene 2). At other times, he expresses bitter sarcasm, showing his undisguised contempt for the hypocrisy, deceit and shallowness with which he is surrounded. He speaks of the king in terms of scornful disgust: he is "a vice of kings," "a villain and a cutpurse," "a king of shreds and patches," a "thing of nothing," who delights in drunkenness and "Keeps wassail, and the swaggering up-spring reels."

During the play-within-the-play and in the presence of the king, Hamlet seems to find some compensation for his inaction in sarcastic remarks: " 'Tis a knavish piece of work; but what o' that? Your Majesty, and we that have free souls, it touches us not; let the galled jade wince, our withers are unwrung." Even the queen is subjected to his sarcasm. Although he dearly loved her once, now his words, like daggers, enter her ears. With cruel irony, he addresses her:

> For who that's but a queen, fair, sober, wise,
> Would from a paddock, from a bat, a gib,
> Such dear concernings hide?

Just before leaving for England, he sarcastically says farewell to Claudius with the words, "Farewell, dear mother." In the graveyard scene, his scorn for all that is false or affected is shown in his sarcastic and ironic allusions to politicians, courtiers and lawyers. Pointing to the skull he holds in his hand, he says:

> Now get you to my lady's chamber, and tell her, let her paint an inch thick, to this favour must she come; make her laught at that.

Refined: He condems the drunkenness of his age (Act I, Scene 4). A man endowed with "noble and most sovereign reason," he usually associates with scholars and artists. He composes verses, and carries memorandum books with him. He possesses "The courtier's, soldier's, scholar's eye, tongue, sword" and was:

> The expectancy and rose of the fair state,
> The glass of fashion and the mould of form,
> The observed of all observers.

His mind inclines toward meditation and philosophy, and the emotional side of his character is as highly developed as the intellectual. His sensitive conscience and intellect account for much of his irresolution. To the gravedigger, he is mad, but to Horatio, he is "a noble heart." He is deeply hurt by his mother's lack of shame and modesty, and the king's falseness and lust are more revolting to Hamlet than the crime of murder.

Question 22.

What may be gathered from the play about Hamlet's personal appearance?

Answer

Ophelia, lamenting Hamlet's transformation, describes him as having been:

> The expectancy and rose of the fair state,
> The glass of fashion and the mould of form,
> The observed of all observers.

This description leads us to imagine a noble, youthful physical form, dignified and graceful in action, with commanding voice. His interesting personality is made still more interesting by the cloud of melancholy hanging over him and the proud and scornful manner that he sometimes assumes. But it is difficult to reconcile this ideal picture with the one that presents itself in the fifth act, when the queen describes him as "*fat*, and scant of breath." In order to reconcile the queen's statement with the ideal impression, "hot" and "faint" have been suggested as possible alterations of the text.

Question 23.

What do we learn from the play concerning the customs of the stage in Shakespeare's time?

Answer

From Hamlet's conversation with Rosencrantz and Guildenstern in the second act, we learn that children had been recently introduced upon the stage and that they were made to ridicule the regular actors. Because of the children's popularity, the regular actors, the "Tragedians of the city," had been compelled to travel from town to town. From a reference, in the same act, to a "cracked voice," we learn that female parts were played by boys (Act II, Scene 2, 427-8). Hamlet's instructions to the players (Act III, Scene 2) teach us that there were certain acting tendencies that, in Shakespeare's opinion, required reform. The extravagant movements, gestures and speech of certain actors, and the buffoonery of the clowns, who would "themselves laugh, to set on some quantity of barren spectators to laugh, too, though in the meantime some necessary question of the play be then to be considered," are criticized. Other items of information about the Elizabethan stage to be gathered from the play are that actors wore wigs and that plays were acted at universities, with amateurs taking part.

Question 24.

What terms of condemnation does Hamlet, on different occasions, use to describe Polonius?

Answer

At the first meeting between Hamlet and Polonius, the prince calls the lord chamberlain a fishmonger. Then, he questions his honesty and, on parting from him, refers to him and others like him as "tedious old fools." When Polonius re-enters, Hamlet describes him to Rosencrantz and Guildenstern as a "great baby, not yet out of his swaddling-clouts (clothes)." To Ophelia, Hamlet says, within the hearing of her father, "Let the doors be shut upon him, that he may play the fool nowhere but in's own house." Speaking of Polonius' acting experiences, Hamlet, playing upon the words "Capitol" and "capital," calls him a "capital calf." When Hamlet discovers Polonius' body behind the arras, he describes him as a "wretched, rash, intruding fool" and, a little later, as a "foolish, prating knave."

Question 25.

What suggestion can you offer to overcome the awkwardness of the changing of swords in the duel scene?

Answer

After Laertes has hit his rival, Hamlet puts his hand to his side, as though he felt the prick of the unfoiled weapon. Then, just as Laertes is about to take up the foil, which has been knocked out of his hand in the encounter, Hamlet places his foot upon it and, bowing gracefully, presents his antagonist with his own foil.

The change of foils may also be achieved in another way. Hamlet, with his sword, strikes down Laertes' weapon and seizes it with his left hand. At the same instant, Laertes, with his left hand, snatches the foil from the right hand of Hamlet. During the manoeuvre, the combatants change places, and the duel subsequently continues with increased fury.

Question 26.

Show that, in the excitement of the moment and when "desperate with imagination," Hamlet is capable of the deed from which, in his calmer state, his conscience restrains him.

Answer

It has been truly said of Hamlet that he is always

perfectly equal to any call of the moment, but not for one of the future. The ghost had imposed upon him the duty of revenge to be discharged righteously. He was not to taint his mind, nor let his soul contrive against his mother. The consideration of this awful duty turned the current of his thoughts upon religion and immortality. Thus, conscience made a coward of him, and "his native hue of resolution" was "sicklied o'er with the pale cast of thought."

Question 27.

"Suspicion always haunts the guilty mind." How may the truth of this statement be illustrated from the play?

Answer

In her interview with Hamlet, the queen receives a rude shock. The crime she committed in marrying Claudius is, for the first time, exhibited in its true colors. From now on, every trifle seems a prelude to some greater disaster, as she herself says:

> To my sick soul, as sin's true nature is,
> Each toy seems prologue to some great amiss:
> So full of artless jealousy is guilt,
> It spills itself in fearing to be spilt.

But if this is the state of the mind of the queen, what must be the feelings of the king, whose crime was so much greater? How soon he begins to be suspicious of Hamlet is not quite clear, but it is evident that he never attaches much importance to Polonius' theory that love is the sole cause of Hamlet's behavior. What he hears of Hamlet's conversation with Ophelia arouses his fears, and he decides to send the prince to England. During the play-within-the-play, he very soon suspects its motive. "Have you heard the argument? Is there no offence in't?" he asks. Hamlet's answer, "No, no, they do but jest — poison in jest," fails to reassure him. Much as he must have really wished to see the play out to the bitter end, his guilty soul will not allow him to do so. He leaves the hall, in case he should more openly betray his guilt. Now he resolves to hasten Hamlet's departure. He begins to suspect even the queen (Act IV, Scene 1, 1-3). He fears the multitude, and his fears (in this case, probably groundless) cause him to act unwisely in the matter of Polonius' funeral. No longer satisfied to get rid of Hamlet for a time, he now plans to free himself forever from his dangerous enemy. Until then, he says, "Howe'er my haps, my joys were ne'er begun."

Question 28.

Does Shakespeare intend to represent the queen as aware that her husband was murdered?

Answer

There is nothing in the play to show that the queen was aware of the murder of her husband. But there is also no direct proof of her innocence. That Shakespeare did not intend to represent her as having any knowledge of her husband's true means of death appears probable from the following circumstantial evidence:

(1) Her character is weak and incapable of conniving at such a crime as murder.

(2) The ghost makes no reference to her being aware of the murder and bids Hamlet not to pursue her with his vengeance.

(3) During "The Mouse-trap," she watches, unmoved.

(4) When Hamlet acquaints her with the murder of his father, her exclamation implies that she is hearing of it for the first time.

(5) She appears to enter into a conspiracy of silence with Hamlet against Claudius.

(6) The ghost of her husband appears to retain some feeling of affection for her.

(7) Claudius does not dare to allow her to have any suspicion of his scheme for bringing about the death of her son.

Question 29.

Was the madness of Hamlet real or was it an act?

Answer

That Hamlet's madness was an act is proved by the following facts:

(1) His actions are perfectly natural until his interview

with the ghost. After this interview, he warns his companions that he may hereafter "put an antic disposition on."

(2) He appears mad only in the presence of those whom he wishes to deceive. His conduct toward Ophelia, for instance, is a means of alienating her from him.

(3) He talks rationally and with wonderful cleverness and subtlety when speaking to Horatio, his schoolfellows, the players or in soliloquy.

(4) He declares to Rosencrantz and Guildenstern that the king is mistaken in thinking him mad and he begs his mother not to deceive herself by supposing him to be mad. He also offers to prove his sanity to her.

(5) The ghost, which may be supposed to be endowed with supernatural knowledge, on revisiting Hamlet, does not speak to him as to a madman.

Notwithstanding the arguments showing that Hamlet's madness was feigned, there is, nevertheless, no doubt that he was profoundly agitated by a supernatural visitation and by the sense of a responsibility that was too great for his nature to bear. There was certainly disorder in his mind, his disposition having been "horribly shaken with thoughts beyond the reaches of our souls." But his mind never absolutely ceased (except, perhaps, temporarily in the passionate scene with Laertes) to be under the mastery of his will.

Question 30.

Give examples from this drama of plays on words.

Answer

Of the numerous examples of puns that are to be found in this play, the following are some of the most obvious:

1. On *kin* and *kind* (Act I, Scene 2).
2. On three meanings of *tender* (Act I, Scene 3).
3. On *Capitol* and *capital, Brutus* and *Brute* (Act III, Scene 2).
4. On two meanings of *fret* (Act III, Scene 2).
5. On the different meanings of *fine* (Act V, Scene 1).
6. On two meanings of *assurance* (Act V, Scene 1).
7. On two meanings of *lie* and *quick* (Act V, Scene 1).
8. On two meanings of *ground* (Act V, Scene 1).

9. On two meanings of *foil* (Act V, Scene 2).

Question 31.

Refer to some of the chief characteristics of style in *Hamlet.*

Answer

When *Hamlet* (as we have it) was written, Shakespeare had left behind him those early years of authorship when his plays were poems in rhyme and his imagery was mere adornment. He had passed through his period of transition (*Romeo and Juliet, Richard II*), which still showed many marks of immaturity. In *Hamlet*, Shakespeare shows himself a master craftsman, capable of every kind of excellence. The early scenes of the play are remarkable for their rapid dialogue in verse, in which the supernatural is realistically brought into contact with the real. The prose with which the play is liberally interspersed contains several majestic pieces of rhetoric (Act II, Scene 2, 297-312). The soliloquies "are excellent examples of the slow dwelling verse" that is most appropriate to thought in solitude. Like Shakespeare's other plays, *Hamlet* is remarkable for its wealth of imagery, especially for its use of the metaphor. Note Act III, Scene 3, 11-23, where three successive images express the same thought, and Act III, Scene 4, 40-51, where the metaphors "are flaming apparitions, which are like a picture in a flash of lightning."

Question 32.

Sketch briefly the character of Polonius.

Answer

Polonius is the adviser of the king, whom he serves, to the best of his ability, loyally and enthusiastically. He possesses a certain amount of the confidence of the king, who, however, consults him more often upon domestic than upon state affairs. As a result of his long experience, he has acquired a considerable share of worldly wisdom, which he is fond of exhibiting on all occasions, whether appropriate or not. The king thinks of him "as of a man faithful and honourable." The queen speaks of him as a "good old man." Laertes' love for him is such that, to avenge his death, he "hazards both the worlds," and Ophelia, in her madness, retains only the sweetest memories of him.

This is the light in which he is regarded by those whom natural affection blinded to his defects, or by people who see in him a means of serving their own ends. Hamlet, however, brings an unbiased judgment to bear upon his character. Hamlet is not much mistaken in his unfavorable opinion of the "wretched, rash, intruding foot," as the following considerations will prove:

(1) Polonius is deceitful and cunning, as is shown by the indirect, crooked methods he adopts for obtaining any information he needs. He sets spies upon his son's actions in Paris, uses his daughter as an instrument for discovering the cause of Hamlet's madness and is not above playing the eavesdropper.

(2) He is suspicious and prying, meddles with everything, listens to slander about his daughter, mistrusts his son and boasts to the king of his ability to find "where truth is hid, though it were hid, indeed, within the centre."

(3) He is superficial, shallow, conceited and talkative. He prides himself upon his knowledge and perception, as well as his literary, critical and acting ability. All the while, however, he is exposing his own folly and ignorance.

(4) He is ignorant of true wisdom and entirely misunderstands Hamlet's nature and actions. He violates good taste even while promoting it. He is, in fact, one of those "seeming wise men," of whom it has been said that they "may make shift to get opinion, but let no man choose them for employment."

Question 33.

Review the different meetings between Hamlet and Rosencrantz and Guildenstern. What is the purpose and the result of each of them?

Answer

The first meeting takes place in the lobby, just after Hamlet has been ridiculing Polonius. The object of the courtiers is to learn from Hamlet the cause of his strangeness. The attempt results in Hamlet's discovering the errand upon which they have been sent and declaring that his "uncle-father and aunt-mother" are deceived in supposing him to be mad.

Their next appearance before Hamlet is merely for the purpose of informing him of the king's willingness to hear the play. Having performed their errand, they leave immediately to make the players hurry.

After the play, they announce to Hamlet that his mother wishes to speak to him in her chamber. They attempt, by open questions, to draw from Hamlet the cause of his behavior and, again, leave baffled.

Afterward, the King sends them to Hamlet to find out where the body of Polonius is and to take it to the chapel. Having failed in their errand, they return, with Hamlet to the king.

Question 34.

Show how tragic force is given to the last scene of *Hamlet.* Explain the effect of three significant developments earlier in the play upon the principal events of this scene.

Answer

The last scene of Hamlet is full of tragic force. Most of the tragedy results from the death of Hamlet, the noblest member of the Danish court. He was "the glass of fashion and the mould of form. The rose and th' expectancy of the fair state." Although it could be foreseen that his delay in carrying out his revenge upon King Claudius could come to no good, he is so "free from all contriving" that this nemesis seems too harsh a punishment for him. When we see that Horatio, who is a most noble and wise man, is willing to die with his friend, we must admire Hamlet for the fact that he has, and is worthy of, such a true friend, whom he "has grappled to his soul with hoops of steel."

The death of Queen Gertrude seems tragic, too. Although she is weak and lets Claudius influence her, she has been a loving mother to Hamlet, and there is much in her that is lovable. Although Hamlet calls her a "most pernicious woman" and "most seeming-virtuous," she loves Hamlet deeply and "has screened much heat between him and the king."

The fact that both characters are killed by treachery, plotting and "wanton murder" deepens the tragedy. Hamlet's failure to "sweep to his revenge," after the ghost's revelation of the murder, allows Claudius to live and trap Hamlet with plots that finally bring him to ruin.

Hamlet is "free from all contriving" and doubts the ghost's truthfulness. Therefore, he resolves to stage "The Mouse-Trap" before Claudius and watch his reaction to it. Claudius' "occult guilt" is revealed, and Hamlet says that now he could "drink hot blood and do such bitter business as the day would quake to look upon." Yet he thinks too "precisely on the event'' and fails to kill Claudius while the king is praying. Again, Claudius is left alive to bring about Hamlet's death.

The impulsive killing of Polonius, who, although "a wretched, rash, intruding fool,'' was the principal statesman in Denmark, leads to Laertes' hasty voyage to Denmark to seek vengeance. Ophelia becomes mad after her father's death, and her drowning so upsets Laertes that he becomes a willing tool in Claudius' hands. He readily agrees to use poison and treachery to kill the unsuspecting Hamlet.

NOTES

NOTES

NOTES

NOTES

NOTES

NOTES